1001 Hideous history FACTS

1001 Hideous history FACTS

Alex Woolf

Delve into the depths of our despicable past!

ARCTURUS

ARCTURUS

This edition published in 2008 by Arcturus Publishing Limited
26/27 Bickels Yard, 151–153 Bermondsey Street,
London SE1 3HA

ISBN: 978-1-84858-007-7

Printed in Singapore

Author: Alex Woolf

Goblin illustrations by Steve Beaumont

Editor: Kate Overy

CONTENTS

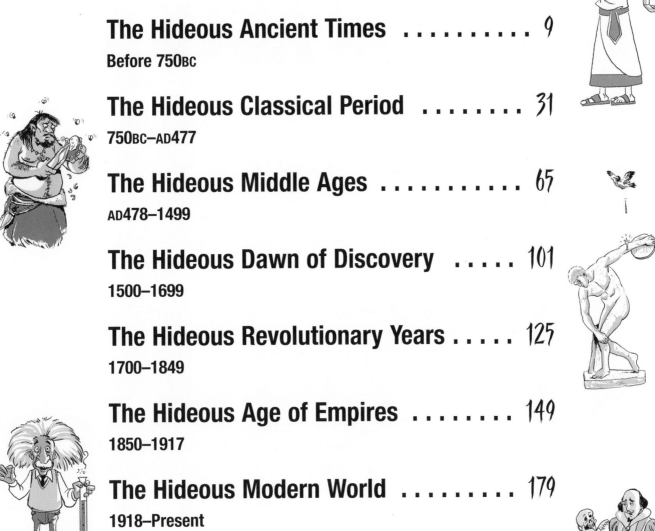

The Putrid Past

Are you concentrating? Then get ready for the most hideous history lesson of your life! Learn just how disgusting, dirty and despicable our ancestors really were! From the ancient times to the Middle Ages to the modern world – each era in history has its own frightful facts to share. So if you're having a particularly rotten day, just think about poor old Richard Raker who, in 1326, fell into a cesspit and 'drowned monstrously in his own excrement'.

Yes, life was pretty hard for most people, what with famine, plague, war, cannibalism and the poor state of plumbing. And if people weren't having a tough enough time coping with all of that, there was always some revolting ruler eager to heap further miseries on them. The Mongol leader, Tamerlane, for example, once ordered a tower to be constructed out of bricks, mortar… and living men!

Revolting Rulers

However, no one – not even kings, queens and leaders – could escape the utter beastliness of history. Here are a few free facts (not part of your 1001 total) listing some particularly nasty ways that historical leaders have come to a sticky end:

After being defeated in battle, the Roman emperor Valerian was used as a footstool before being skinned alive and stuffed with dung.

Anglo-Saxon King of England, Harold II died in the Battle of Hastings when he was shot in the eye with an arrow.

Adolph Frederick of Sweden is known as 'the king who ate himself to death'. He died after stuffing himself with lobster, caviar, smoked herring, champagne and 14 servings of his favourite dessert.

Delve in!

Arguably, the most amazing thing about human history is how, amid all this dreadfulness – extraordinary things were achieved over the years. We have to admire Heron of Alexandria, for example, who invented the steam engine 17 centuries before it was even needed. And the Chinese invention of the 'excrement bomb' in 1044 is certainly not to be sniffed at!

So, if you're brave enough to be disgusted, repulsed and shocked by the acts of our appalling ancestors... read on!

Don't let history repeat itself!

After reading this book you might feel like testing out Stone Age man's toilet paper made from moss… or making yourself your own portable lavatory like King Henry VIII. What you mustn't do is try to recreate the horrors of our putrid past – leave all those appalling acts to our ancestors! Read on and revel in this revolting collection of historical facts and be glad your future's happy, not hideous!

The Hideous Ancient Times

Before 750BC

Archaeologists study *coprolites* (fossilized faeces) to find out what people, animals and even dinosaurs used to eat. Coprolites can even reveal any worms or parasites people had in the Stone Age.

Wooly mammoths had a large, hairy flap of skin that covered their bottom to keep them warm!

The world's oldest building is a primitive shelter built in Japan around 498,000BC. It was discovered in the year 2000 – it must have been a bit smelly by then!

Some of the earliest human populations lived in South-east Asia. Tragically most life in this region was wiped out by the eruption of a massive volcano on the island of Toba 74,000 years ago.

The paint used to make cave paintings was made from blood or animal fat mixed with mineral or plant pigments.

By 20,000BC people had worked out that an easy way to get lots of food at once was to drive animals off a cliff to kill them in one go. Remains of 100,000 horses have been found at the bottom of a cliff in France. That was probably more than they could eat in one sitting!

The oldest maps of the stars can be found on cave walls in France and Spain and were painted 16,500 years ago. Stars inside the outline of a bull are those in the constellation now known as Taurus – the bull!

14,000 years ago, Native Americans in Florida impaled tortoises on sticks and roasted them, like kebabs, over a fire.

In South America around 12,000 years ago, there were beavers the size of donkeys and sloths the size of elephants. Freaky!

The last ice age ended around 10,000 years ago.

A dog burial ground from the Stone Age in Sweden, has dogs buried with 'grave goods' (objects to help them in the afterlife) just like their owners.

People living in Jericho in 7500BC took ancestor-worship to the extreme! They'd remove the head of a dead grandparent, fill it with clay, paint the skull to look like flesh and place shells in the eye sockets for eyes.

Prehistoric doctors in many areas set broken bones by holding the limb in position and covering it with clay-rich river mud. The cast could be broken later, when the bone had healed.

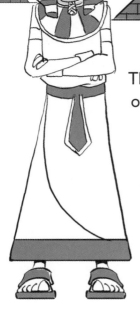

The pyramids of Egypt are the oldest of the seven wonders of the ancient world, and the only one still surviving.

The *Chinchorro* (an ancient Peruvian fishing community) made the oldest mummies known to man, dating back to 6000BC. Chinchorro mummies were repainted regularly then taken along to special ceremonies and events.

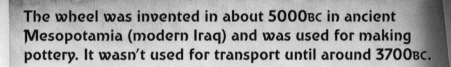

The wheel was invented in about 5000BC in ancient Mesopotamia (modern Iraq) and was used for making pottery. It wasn't used for transport until around 3700BC.

In Jericho around 7,000 years ago, people buried their dead under the dirt floor of their houses.

Woodhenge in Wiltshire, England, was originally a circle of wooden posts built around 4000BC. It's believed to have been a sacrificial site as bodies have been discovered, buried in the centre.

The first false teeth were used in China and India 6,000 years ago.

The oldest mummified head is called *Chulina* and was found in the Andes in South America.

A study has shown that prehistoric Americans began spicing up their food with hot chillies 6,000 years ago!

It was the ancient Egyptians who devised the first 365-day calendar. The earliest recorded year in human history is 4236BC.

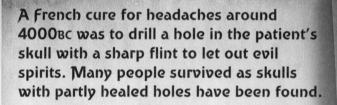

A French cure for headaches around 4000BC was to drill a hole in the patient's skull with a sharp flint to let out evil spirits. Many people survived as skulls with partly healed holes have been found.

A tomb in Ireland contains the oldest known map of the moon – it's 5,000 years old. Leonardo da Vinci made the next map of the moon in around 1505.

Arabian explorers thought that the sticky resin on mummies' bandages was a type of oil that they called *mummiyah*, which is how the mummies got their name.

Ancient Egyptians believed that if a body was allowed to rot, the person wouldn't be able to reach the afterlife.

The earliest known murder victim was a man who had lived in the Italian Alps around 3300BC. His body, found in 1991, was preserved in ice with an arrowhead in his back.

When dead pharaohs were embalmed in ancient Egypt, the brain was hooked out through the nose or scooped through an eye socket. Often, the brain was chopped up with a wire first to make it easier to get out.

Writing is thought to have been invented in 3200BC in Mesopotamia.

The ancient Egyptians had dental drills and were able to drill out decayed parts of teeth, but they are not known to have had any anaesthetic to help the patient deal with the pain. Ouch!

A pit containing the bones of animals eaten in prehistoric Russia also contained human bones, leading archaeologists to think early people in the area were cannibals.

The final stage of embalming a body was to press a decorated golden 'death mask' over the mummy's face, so that when the pharaoh's spirit returned to the tomb, he would recognize his body.

The ancient Assyrians had a habit of *flaying* (skinning) their enemies alive and hanging up their skins outside the city wall.

People in Mesopotamia believed in demons called *lilu* who were the spirits of people who had died unmarried. They came into homes looking for victims to marry them in the demon world.

Hundreds of bodies are burried under Stonehenge (a prehistoric monument in Wiltshire, England) but they aren't thought to have been human sacrifices. It's believed the site was used as a cemetery before the stones were put up.

In ancient Egypt, a nobleman's worth included the value of his male servents and his cows – but not female servants – they were worth less than cows!

Pharaoh Hor-Aha who reigned around 3050BC, was killed by a hippopotamus while he was on a hunting expedition.

Babylonian king Hammurabi was tough on unreliable builders. If a house collapsed due to poor workmanship and killed the owner, the builder was executed.

One way that archaeologists find out what people ate in ancient times is by examining food found in the stomachs of bog people.

The first drink driving conviction occurred in about 2800BC. A drunk Egyptian charioteer was arrested after running over a priestess. He was nailed to the door of a tavern and his corpse remained hanging there as a warning to others.

Stone age people used moss as toilet paper!

Tea was discovered in 2737BC by Emperor Shennong of China, who was also known as 'The Divine Farmer'.

Before embalming the body, a pharaoh's vital organs (the lungs, liver, stomach and intestines) were removed and stored in special jars in the tomb.

Mummies were entombed with their mouths open so they could eat in the afterlife.

If a peasant didn't work hard enough in ancient Egypt, he would be whipped or have a toe or finger cut off.

Queen Puabi of Mesopotamia died around 2600BC. Her grave contains the bodies of five armed guards and 23 ladies in waiting. The lucky servants were poisoned so they could accompany their queen to the next world.

Many mummies had black shiny stones put in their eye sockets, but pharoah Rameses IV had small onions instead!

Pharaoh Djoser's 'step' pyramid, built in 2620BC, covered 150,000 square metres (1,614,586 square feet) of desert – the same as 21 football pitches!

Some mummies have up to 20 layers of wrappings, stretching to hundreds of metres of cloth.

The Great Pyramid of Giza was built over a 20-year period, finishing in about 2560BC. It used 2,400,000 blocks of stone weighing a total of 6.3 million tonnes (13,889 million pounds)!

The ancient Egyptians kissed with their noses instead of their lips.

Traders around the Dead Sea in Israel used to sell a gluey black substance called *bitumen* (produced by the sea) to the ancient Egyptians, for them to use in mummification.

In the 'opening of the mouth' ceremony, a priest would touch a mummy's mouth with an axe and with a chisel, rub its face with milk and hug the bandaged corpse. People believed the dead man could then eat, drink and move!

Ur-Nammu, a Mesopotamian ruler of about 2050BC, died in battle when his chariot got stuck in the mud and he fell off.

An ancient Egyptian cure for blindness was the mashed eyeball of a pig mixed with honey and *red ochre* (a coloured pigment) poured into the ear.

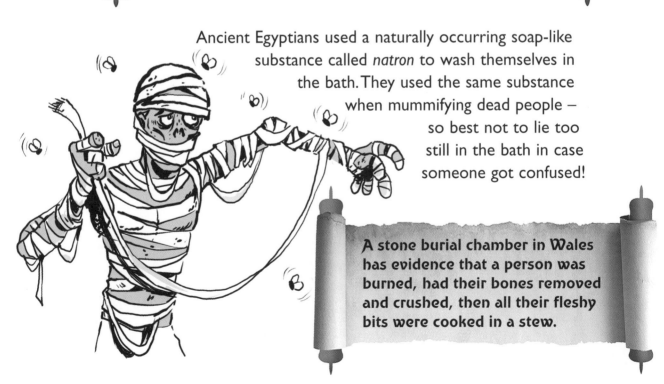

Ancient Egyptians used a naturally occurring soap-like substance called *natron* to wash themselves in the bath. They used the same substance when mummifying dead people – so best not to lie too still in the bath in case someone got confused!

A stone burial chamber in Wales has evidence that a person was burned, had their bones removed and crushed, then all their fleshy bits were cooked in a stew.

The longest reigning monarch in history was Pepy II, who ruled Egypt for **94 years** (2278–2184BC).

The first evidence of soap is a recipe written on a Babylonian clay tablet dating from 2200BC. The formula explains how to make soap consisting of water, alkali and cassia oil. Until then, people were just really, really dirty!

The ancient Egyptians played an early kind of ten-pin bowling, using large stones set up as pins, and smaller stones as balls.

Tyrian purple, a dye used by royalty from around 2000BC, was made from slime produced by a rare sea snail. It took 8,500 snails to produce just one gram of dye!

Hundreds of thousands of mummified animals have been found buried in tombs including cats, birds, fish, snakes and even crocodiles!

Our division of minutes and hours into units of 60 comes from the *sexagesimal* (sixty-based) numeral system first devised by the Sumerians in the 2nd century BC.

When a pharaoh died, it's believed that his heart was weighed against a feather carrying all his lies and crimes. If the two sides of the scales balanced, the pharaoh could enter paradise. Otherwise a monster would eat his soul and he'd be lost forever. Sounds fair...

The world's oldest continuously inhabited city is Damascus in Syria, which has been occupied since at least 2000BC.

After removing the innards and stuffing the body with natron, a mummy-in-the-making was left to dry out for 70 days before wrapping. It was then stuffed with linen and straw to keep its shape – the pharaoh wouldn't want to turn up in the afterlife looking all saggy!

The earliest example of musical notation was found on a clay tablet in Mesopotamia dating from around 1800BC.

Some ancient Egyptians slept on pillows made of stone. Comfy!

In 1750BC, the Babylonian king Hammurabi established a particularly harsh set of laws. Punishments included cutting off a finger or hand for theft and cutting off a man's lower lip for kissing a married woman.

When a king died in ancient China thousands of slaves and prisoners of war could be sacrificed as a display of respect, and an offering to god.

Careless embalmers accidentally wrapped flies, lizards and even a mouse into some mummies' bandages!

In 1580BC, pharoah Apophis of Upper Egypt sent this message to pharoah Sekenenre of Lower Egypt: 'The farting of the hippopotami swimming in the temple pool at your palace is keeping me awake. Do something about it or else!' Apophis' palace was over 640 kilometres (397 miles) away, so Sekenenre took this as an insult and immediately declared war.

It is thought that pharaoh Seqenenre, who reigned around 1550BC was killed in battle. His mummified corpse has head wounds from an axe, a spear, a club and a dagger. There's nothing like making sure...

The ancient Egyptians believed that onions would keep bad spirits away. The neighbours too, perhaps!

When the troops of pharaoh Thutmose I invaded Syria in 1525BC, they were astonished to encounter rain for the first time. Rain was unheard of in Egypt; they described it as 'the river Nile falling from the sky'.

'Oracle bones' were used in ancient China to predict the future. They were made from pieces of animal bone or shell but sometimes human bones were used instead...

Stone Age Australian men often had their two front teeth removed as a sign of being tough and manly.

The earliest death sentence is recorded on an ancient Egyptian scroll from about 1500BC. A teenage male, convicted of 'magic' was sentenced to kill himself either by poison or stabbing. Executioners were a bit lazy back then.

The Olmec people of Mexico began growing cocoa beans and making chocolate around 1500BC.

Pharaoh Thutmosis III (1479-1425BC) was a generous monarch. He once made a single offering of 13.5 tonnes (29,762 pounds) of gold to the Temple of Amun at Thebes.

Some Egyptian mummies show evidence of tapeworms. The tapeworms were not mummified separately!

Remains found in a mass grave in Dakota, USA, show that prehistoric warriors scalped their victims, probably to keep the hair as a trophy.

According to legend, when pharaoh Amenhotep (1427–1400BC) defeated a rebellion in Nubia, southern Egypt, he killed 312 people in a single hour and took home the right hands of all his victims.

In the 13th century BC, Chinese priests would write questions to their gods on a tortoise shell, then place a hot iron on the shell. The way the shell cracked gave them the answer to their question.

Ancient Egyptian women put a cone of perfumed fat on their heads. As it melted in the daytime heat it made their hair smell nice. It can't have looked very nice though!

Moses, an early Hebrew ruler, believed in matching punishments to crimes. His laws of 1300BC were summarized as 'an eye for an eye and a tooth for a tooth'.

The first instance of biological warfare may have been a terrible plague that struck the Hittites (an ancient Syrian civilization) in 1335BC. It's thought that the Hittites' enemies introduced *tularemia* (a deadly animal disease) by sending them infected rams.

The ancient Egyptians offered mummified animals to the gods. Some conartists sold pretend mummies for this purpose, that were really just bandages filled with twigs and sawdust!

In 1294BC pharaoh Ramses II was defeated by the Hittites at the Battle of Kadesh. He went on to erect a memorial to his magnificent 'victory' anyway!

The earliest known unit of length was used by ancient British tomb builders in around 2300BC. The name of the unit is unknown but its length was about 83 centimetres (32.67 inches).

By the time pharaoh Ramses II died in 1225BC, he had fathered 96 sons and 60 daughters. That's a lot of birthday presents to buy…

Pharaoh Pepy II of Egypt always kept several naked slaves with him whose bodies were smeared with honey. This encouraged flies to land on them instead of on him! A very sticky business…

By Babylonian king Hammurabi's law, stealing from a burning house meant you would be burned alive, and charging too much for a drink was punishable by drowning!

When pharaoh Rameses II was mummified in 1212BC, the embalmers tried to keep his nose in shape by stuffing it with peppercorns!

The granite lid of Tutankhamun's sarcophagus weighed over 1,250 kilograms (2,755 pounds) – that's about as much as 13 large men!

When the Nile failed to flood in the period 1073–1064BC there was a great famine in Egypt and people resorted to eating each other.

Ancient Egyptians treated some infections with mouldy bread. As it happens, the mould on bread contains antibiotics, so it probably worked.

Some tomb robbers made fast work of robbing Egyptian tombs by setting fire to the contents. The wood and fabric would burn away then the hidden gold melted and formed pools. When the fire had died down and the gold had cooled, the robbers could pick up puddles of solid gold!

Using primitive ships and no navigational aids, the Polynesians managed to locate virtually all the tiny islands spread over 14 million square kilometres (nearly 5.5 million square miles) of the Pacific Ocean, claiming all of them as their own.

Pharoah Amenhotep was like an Egyptian superhero. He is said to have single-handedly killed seven rebellious princes in battle, he could row six times as far as 200 men and beat anyone in a drinking contest!

Stonehenge may be a giant calendar. On the summer solstice (21 June), the rising sun is perfectly aligned with the stone circle.

Many of the early discoverers of mummies believed they possessed magical healing powers. Mummy wrappings were ground up and sold as a magic powder to put on wounds or to swallow as a cure for various ailments. Mmm... tasty.

Australian aborigines have used kangaroo-skin bandages for thousands of years.

The earliest recorded mention of cheesecake was in 776BC, when it was served to athletes competing in the first Olympic games.

Traces of tobacco and cocoa have been found in mummy wrappings – plants not known outside the Americas before the Europeans arrived there in the 16th century! Perhaps the Egyptians got there first...

The Hideous Classical Period

750 BC – AD 477

Ancient Romans spread pigeon droppings on their hair to lighten it – the ammonia acted as a bleach. You wouldn't have wanted to work in a hairdresser's in those days...

The world's oldest monarchy is the Imperial House of Japan, said to have been established on 11 February 660BC.

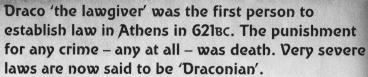

Draco 'the lawgiver' was the first person to establish law in Athens in 621BC. The punishment for any crime – any at all – was death. Very severe laws are now said to be 'Draconian'.

The Greek athlete Protiselaus hurled a discus 46.3 metres (151.9 feet) around 600BC. His record stood until 1928, when American athlete Clarence Houser managed 47.2 metres (154.8 feet).

The philosopher Heraclitus (535–475BC) tried to cure himself of *dropsy* (a disease which causes water on the lungs) by burying himself in a pile of cow dung. It didn't work. He just died smelly.

Under the Roman king Tarquinius Priscus, people who committed suicide were crucified... even though they were already dead!

Ancient Greeks didn't use napkins. Instead they wiped their hands on pieces of bread, then fed the bread to the dogs.

Despite his harsh laws, Draco of Athens was very popular. Attending a reception one day, he was showered with hats, shirts and cloaks by admiring citizens. By the time they dug him out from under the clothing he had been smothered to death.

Roman doctors didn't use anaesthetics when they fixed broken bones or cut off rancid arms and legs. Instead, they were trained not to take any notice of the screams!

Alcmaeon of Croton, Greece, is the first person known to have studied the human body by cutting up corpses, around 520BC.

The Celts, who lived in Britain around 500BC, collected the heads of people they slaughtered in battle. They stuck them on poles, chucked them in rivers as gifts to the gods, nailed them to the walls as decorations or hollowed them out to use as cups. You'd think their drinks would run out through the eyeholes…

It's thought that Greek mathematician Pythagoras was beaten to death by an angry mob around 500BC. He could have run away but he would have had to trample through a field of beans. Pythagoras believed that beans held the souls of dead ancestors, so he chose to die.

Ancient Romans believed the souls of the dead needed the odd human sacrifice. When someone died, it was the custom to spill human blood over their grave or tomb. Lazy slaves were often chosen as a sacrifice.

The first ever 'marathon' was run by a Greek messenger called Pheidippides in 490BC. He ran 42 kilometres (26 miles) from a town called Marathon to Athens to announce that the Greeks had beaten the Persians in a battle. As soon as he got there, he collapsed and died from exhaustion.

The Persian king, Xerxes, wanted to get a large army over the river Hellespont so he built a bridge. When a storm destroyed the bridge, Xerxes was so angry, he punished the river by having a soldier whip it and throw shackles into it!

Spartans held whipping competitions. Whoever could stand the most whipping without making a fuss would win. You could even win if you died, but it wasn't as much fun.

During the siege of Megara, Greece, the Megarians poured oil over a herd of pigs, set fire to them, then drove the pigs towards the war elephants of their enemies. The elephants bolted in terror from the squealing pigs and trampled the enemy soldiers.

A well preserved bog man with six fingers was discovered in England. The man had been killed as a sacrifice in early Roman times.

The Greek playwright, Aeschylus, died when an eagle dropped a tortoise on his head. The eagle apparently thought his bald head was a rock that it could crack the tortoise on!

Early Romans used porcupine quills as toothpicks.

The largest naval battle of ancient times was the Battle of Salamis in 480BC when 371 Greek ships defeated 1,271 Persian ships. Around 200,000 soldiers and sailors are thought to have fought.

Hippocrates (460–357BC) was a great doctor for his time, though he wouldn't pass his medical exams today. To help him work out what was wrong with patients, he'd taste whatever came out of their body – including urine, earwax, vomit and snot!

To clean themselves, Romans poured olive oil all over their bodies then scraped off the oily, dirty gunk with a curved blade called a *strigil*. Yuk.

In 435BC, the Greek philosopher Anaxagoras was kicked out of Athens for suggesting that the sun was not just a glowing circle of light but a big ball of fire.

In ancient Rome, urine was collected from public toilets and used as a clothes dye, a hair product and an ingredient in toothpaste.

A terrible plague killed a third of the population of Athens in 430BC. Victims had a fever, headaches, stomach pain, vomiting, diarrhoea and were covered in painful blisters. Those that didn't die often lost fingers, toes or their sight. Historians still don't know what the disease was.

The play *Hecuba* written in 424BC by Euripides contains the first known criticism of slavery – it didn't make much difference, as the Greeks continued to keep huge numbers of slaves.

The ancient Egyptians used trained dogs to catch thieves, runaway slaves and tax evaders.

In 400BC the Greek city of Sparta had just 25,000 citizens and 500,000 slaves. That's 20 slaves each!

When the Egyptian general Phanes swapped sides in a war and joined the enemy Persians, the angry Egyptians killed his sons and drank their blood.

In 356BC, Herostratus set fire to the temple of Artemis just so that his name would go down in history. The Greek government executed him and didn't write his name in the official records. That didn't work though, as we still know Herostratus did it!

The Chinese lord Shang (died 338BC) ordered everyone in the country to spy on each other. People were divided into groups of five or ten and had to report any offences. If they failed to report a crime, they were cut in half.

The Greek philosopher Aristotle was the first person to discover that dolphins are mammals not fish, in about 340BC.

In 320BC, the Egyptians attacked the city of Jerusalem on the Sabbath (the Jewish day of rest). The Jewish people couldn't fight back, so the city was taken without a struggle.

In Kazakhstan around 300BC a woman had her left foot amputated and replaced with two bones taken from a ram – the first attempt at a limb transplant.

The most successful textbook of all time is Euclid's *Elements*, written in about 300BC. It has gone through more than 1,000 editions since the invention of printing.

The Greek playwright Philemon (362–262BC) laughed so hard at one of his own jokes that he died laughing!

The Chinese emperor Qin (259–210BC) was ruthless. Anyone who disobeyed him or argued against his rules was set to work building the Great Wall of China or buried alive.

The first known food-fight was between the Greek mathematician Archimedes and the Egyptian king Ptolemy III around 250BC. When the king questioned Archimedes' work on geometry, the mathematician began pelting the king with olives. Ptolemy's guards then threw fruit at Archimedes, forcing him to surrender.

The punishment for killing a close relative in ancient Rome was to be sewn into a sack with a dog, a snake, a cockerel and a monkey and thrown into the river Tiber.

The ancient Greek mathematician Archimedes used mirrors to focus sunlight on enemy ships so that they burst into flames. His super weapon was known as *Archimedes' death ray*.

Ancient Egyptian priests removed all hair from their bodies, including their eyelashes and eyebrows!

A Greek cure for bad breath was to boil the head of a hare together with three mice and rub the resulting mixture on your gums. It probably covered up the original smell, but wasn't necessarily any better!

In 230BC, Greek philosopher Eratosthenes worked out the earth's circumference by studying shadows cast by the sun in both Alexandria and Syene on the longest day of the year.

The first emperor of China, Qin Shi Huang (221–210BC), built a network of 270 palaces, all linked by tunnels. He was so scared of being assassinated that he slept in a different palace every night.

In 215BC the Roman invasion of Syracuse was stopped by an ingenious machine invented by the mathematician Archimedes. A giant crane called *The Claws of Archimedes* was used to pluck Roman ships out of the water and smash them against the rocks.

In 213BC, Qin Shi Huang ordered that all China's books be burned. A few brave scholars risked their lives and managed to save some.

Roman women were expected to be hair-free, removing the hair under their arms and on their legs. One recipe for hair remover included powdered snake and the blood of a wild goat.

In 212BC, officers of the Chinese chancellor Li Si collected 460 of the country's greatest scholars and had them all buried alive in a mass grave. It wasn't a good time to admit to being really clever!

Some Ancient Greek buildings had communal toilets – a long marble bench with holes that people sat on. The waste flowed into a running stream.

When the first emperor of China died in 210BC, an army of 7,500 terracotta soldiers was placed in his tomb at Xianyang. It was also booby-trapped, so that anyone who tried to break through the hillside doorway would be shot with an arrow.

Greek mathematician Archimedes was hard at work on a maths problem when a messenger arrived from the Roman commander Marcellus. Archimedes waved the soldier away, and in a fit of anger the soldier killed him.

Marcus Licinius Crassus (115–53BC) was one of the wealthiest men in Rome. He made his fortune by accusing his rivals of treason and then taking their money as a punishment for their 'crimes'.

Both the Greeks and Romans believed they could tell the future by examining the pattern made by the guts spilled from a sacrificed bird. The future always looked grim for birds…

Spartacus led a lot of revolting slaves (slaves who were rebelling, not slaves who didn't wash) against the Romans who owned them. He died in battle but 6,600 of his followers were crucified in rows lining the Appian Way, a main road that led to Rome.

It took over 1,700 years to build the Great Wall of China. It was built entirely by slaves and other forced labourers. They were fed just enough to keep them alive and many died of accidents, disease and exhaustion. The Chinese say that each brick in the wall represents a life lost.

The only rule in Roman wrestling matches was never to poke the eyes of your opponent.

A Roman remedy for baldness was a mixture of pigeon droppings, cumin, horseradish and beetroot or stinging nettles. Ouch!

Marcus Licinius Crassus of Rome had his own private firefighting force. When fire broke out, he forced people living nearby to sell their houses to him. Only then would he send in his firefighters to extinguish the flames.

Several of Aristotle's writings survived purely by chance. Some old documents found in a dirty pit around 80BC turned out to be the only copies of his works.

King Mithridates VI of Pontus took small doses of poison throughout his life to build up his resistance in case someone tried to poison him. His plan backfired when he was captured by the Romans in 63BC. He tried to kill himself using poison but it had no effect! Instead he got a slave to kill him with a sword.

Gladiatorial games were first held at funerals. The Romans believed that spilling blood on their grave would help the dead person get to heaven.

Both the Greeks and the Romans played a game called *knucklebones*. It was played with little cubic bones taken from the feet of animals such as sheep or goats. You had to throw the bones in the air and catch them in different ways on one hand. The game wasn't popular with sheep or goats…

Many Celtic graves contain the bodies of an old person and several younger people. Archaeologists think the younger people were killed as a sacrifice to keep the old person company. That's taking visiting elderly relatives to extremes!

A sumptuous feast in ancient Greece might include any of these yummy morsels: sea urchins; thrushes; peacock eggs; grasshoppers or a pig that had died from eating too much.

The Romans' worst defeat was in 53BC when just 10,000 soldiers of the Parthian army in Turkey beat their 40,000-strong army.

Wealthy Roman, Marcus Licinius Crassus, was killed by his enemies who poured molten gold down his throat.

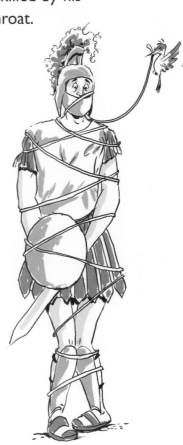

Cleopatra once spent ten million *sesterces* (silver and bronze coins) on one dinner! The food was very ordinary, but the second course was a cup of strong vinegar into which she dissolved one of her priceless pearl earrings.

When Julius Caesar besieged the town of Avaricum in northern France, the army of Gauls held out for 25 days. But when it rained, they ran for cover and the Romans stormed the town. Of the 40,000 people there, only 800 survived the onslaught of the angry (wet) Romans.

The longest year on record was 46BC – the year Julius Caesar introduced his new calendar. As well as adding two extra months, he had to create 23 additional days in February to make up the difference from the previous Egyptian calendar. So 46BC had 455 days rather than the usual 365!

Scythian soldiers had to collect the scalps of people they killed. The scalps were a form of receipt – in exchange for each one they would win a share of the loot after a battle. A soldier with enough scalps could even make a nice cloak from them – very snug!

In Ancient Peru, when a woman found an 'ugly' potato it was the custom for her to mash it into the face of the nearest man.

When Julius Caesar was murdered by his senate in Rome in 44BC, he was stabbed 23 times. It was so crowded and frenzied around Caesar that some of his assailants stabbed each other instead!

After the death of Mark Antony in 30BC, Cleopatra killed herself by allowing a poisonous snake to bite her. Ouch!

The first known railway was in Diolkos, Greece, in the 6th century BC. It was 6 kilometres (3.7 miles) long and carried boats across a narrow strip of land in Corinth. The trucks ran in a grooved limestone track and were pushed by slaves. Working on the railways was much harder in those days!

Wounded Roman soldiers used spiders' webs to help stick their wounds together. They also tucked herbs into their bandages to kill any germs.

The people of Thassos, Greece, built a statue of a famous boxer in the 5th century BC. A jealous opponent attacked the statue, which fell on him and squashed him. The statue was found guilty of murder and thrown into the ocean!

New Scythian soldiers had to drink the blood of the first enemy soldier they killed.

Criminals in Britain in the 5th century BC were thrown (alive) into a swamp known as a *quagmire* to drown.

Philoxenus of Leucas was a legendary glutton of the late 4th century BC. He spent hours hardening his fingers in hot water so he could grab the tastiest hot food from the table before anyone else.

In the 4th century BC, Spartan men were required by law to eat a kilogram (about two pounds) of meat per day to make them braver.

The Roman ceremony of *Lupercalia* was celebrated in February. It involved killing two goats and a dog, then smearing blood from the goats on the foreheads of two young men. Then they had a feast, dressed up in the skins of the dead goats and went around whipping people. They really knew how to party…

The Chinese invented fingerprinting to identify criminals in the 3rd century BC.

The largest monument ever built is the Great Pyramid of Cholula, Mexico. The huge building is more than one third larger than the Great Pyramid of Giza in Egypt. Its construction began in the 1st century BC.

In Teotihuacán, South America, new buildings were dedicated with the help of a human sacrifice. The victim was often a captured enemy warrior who would be killed by having his head cut off, or his heart cut out. Sometimes they didn't bother to kill the sacrifice, they just buried him alive.

In the 3rd century BC, the Romans started worshipping *Terminus,* the god of boundary stones. Moving a boundary marker between towns was punishable by death!

When a criminal was beheaded in ancient Rome, the body was thrown in the river Tiber and the head into the sewers. It gave the body and head a chance to get back together again, as the sewers flowed straight into the river. Only a complete body-and-head combo was allowed into the afterlife.

Vedius Pollio, a rich Roman of the 1st century BC, kept a fish farm at his house where his favourite fish were fed the bodies of dead slaves. It's said that he fed badly behaved slaves to his eels.

Human bodies dumped into bogs are sometimes naturally preserved for thousands of years. When workmen in Cheshire, England, dug up the body of a man, they called the police immediately. It turned out the murder had happened 2000 years ago! He had been sacrificed by the Romans who had smashed his skull into his brain, slit his throat and strangled him.

In Slovakia, in the 1st century BC, 12 people were beaten to death and cut into quarters. Their body parts were then dumped into a pit at a holy site, possibly to ensure a good harvest.

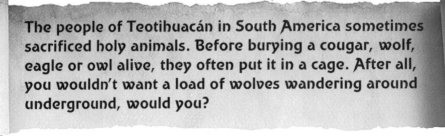

The people of Teotihuacán in South America sometimes sacrificed holy animals. Before burying a cougar, wolf, eagle or owl alive, they often put it in a cage. After all, you wouldn't want a load of wolves wandering around underground, would you?

Boudicca was fearsome Celtic queen who refused to accept Roman rule in Britain. She led her army of thousands into battle with them. In the final clash between the two armies Boudicca was defeated and 80,000 Britons were killed. Only 400 Romans died. Boudicca and her daughters are thought to have poisoned themselves to avoid capture.

The world's first theme park was established near the Italian city of Baia during the 1st century BC. Priests dressed in black robes gave tourists guided tours along the torch-lit passageways!

In Carthage in the 5th century AD, Christian women were catapulted into the air. The crash-landing was their punishment for deciding to be Christians.

By AD15 there were 144 public toilets in Rome – a greater number per person than in most towns today!

For the first seven months of his reign the Roman emperor Caligula (AD37-41) was considered a model emperor. Then he went mad and became ruthlessly cruel.

The Huns, who lived in an area stretching from Germany to Russia, scarred their teenage sons' faces to make them look fiercer when they went into battle.

Emperor Caligula's favourite horse had 18 servants. It was fed oats mixed with gold flakes, lived in a stable made from marble and wore a collar of precious stones!

The Romans used a wet sponge on a stick instead of toilet paper!

In AD37, Roman emperor Caligula became seriously ill and went mad. He executed his loyal followers, banished his wife from Rome and forced his father-in-law and cousin to commit suicide.

Honey-roasted dormouse was a delicacy in ancient Rome. Cooks kept the mice in terracotta jars and fattened them up for a few weeks first to make sure they were extra meaty.

In AD39 Roman emperor Caligula ordered a floating bridge of ships to be built, stretching 3.5 kilometres (2.8 miles) across the Bay of Baiae. A fortune teller had told him that he had no more chance of becoming emperor than of riding a horse across the Bay of Baiae – he managed both.

The Romans report that the Celts used to make a vast, hollow sculpture of a man from branches. They would then fill it with living people and set fire to it to please the gods. They usually used criminals, but if there weren't enough, they picked random innocent people. Unlucky!

Roman emperors were known to feast on such strange delicacies as flamingo tongues, parrotfish livers, roasted suckling puppy and pheasant brain.

Towards the end of his reign, battling with madness, emperor Caligula believed he was a living god and would have conversations with statues of other Roman gods.

Heron of Alexandria invented a steam engine known as an *aeolipile* in AD50, 1,800 years before it was invented in Europe.

To ensure her son Nero became emperor, Agrippina murdered her husband, emperor Claudius, with a plate of poisoned mushrooms in AD54.

When the Romans conquered a land, they made all their young men join the army. Many didn't want to, so the Romans ruled that anyone who didn't fight would be executed. It was better to take a chance than to die for certain!

The Huns used to bind their babies' heads with straps to give their skulls an attractive, elongated shape.

The Roman emperor Nero (AD54–68) kept a 'glutton' – a slave who would eat whatever was put in front of him, including cooked human flesh.

Spartan babies had to look tough from the moment they were born. A baby that looked a bit weak and weedy was either abandoned on a hillside to die or chucked off a cliff.

Some Roman families employed a special educated slave called a *pedagogue* to help teach their children. The pedagogue had a stick with which to beat the child if he didn't work or was naughty. Imagine having a slave employed to hit you with a stick!

Emperor Nero built a giant statue of himself outside his palace. At 30 metres (98 feet) high it was the largest gilded bronze statue in the world. It took 24 elephants to move it!

The Romans used powdered mice brains as toothpaste! No minty-fresh breath in those days then...

In ancient Egypt, you were considered adult at the age of thirteen.

Emperor Nero may have invented ice cream. He sent slaves to the Apennine Mountains to collect snow, which he then flavoured with honey and nuts.

When the British warrior-queen Boudicca marched on the Roman town of *Londinium* (London) her army killed 70,000 people.

The Romans had gods to guard their toilets! Crepitus was god of the toilet and Cloacina was goddess of the public sewer.

Emperor Nero used to watch gladiatorial games with the aid of an emerald – possibly the first recorded use of a lens to help someone see.

According to the Roman writer Tacitus, 50,000 people were killed when a badly built amphitheatre collapsed during a show. The screams of the injured people buried under the rubble could be heard all day and night.

Heron of Alexandria's amazing inventions included: temple doors that opened automatically; the world's first coin-operated vending machine and a mechanical puppet theatre.

Many Roman gladiators became heroic figures with their own fan clubs and huge numbers of followers!

A long flight of stone steps in Rome called the Gemonian Stairs were a bad place to hang out. Several senators and the emperor Vitellius all came to sticky ends there, as it was a favourite spot for assassinations.

The Huns placed slices of raw meat under their saddles so that it cooked as they rode their horses.

The Roman emperor Nero was guilty of many horrible atrocities, even killing his own mother. He made sure the ship she was on sank, then when she swam to safety he sent soldiers to kill her. All that after she'd poisoned her husband for him – how ungrateful!

In AD72, the Romans laid siege to a town in Palestine. When they finally broke through a year later, the Romans discovered that the 936 inhabitants had all killed themselves.

When the volcano Vesuvius erupted in AD79, thousands of people living in the towns of Pompei and Herculaneum were killed. They were scorched by burning winds, crushed under heaps of falling rubble or killed by the fires that swept through the towns.

During the 100 days of the opening games at the Roman amphitheatre, the *Colosseum* in AD80, over 5,000 animals were killed including elephants, tigers, lions, elks, hyenas, hippopotamuses and giraffes.

Saint Ignatius was ripped apart by wild lions as punishment for being a Christian. He was transported from Turkey to Rome around AD100 with ten leopards, and then thrown to the lions in the amphitheatre.

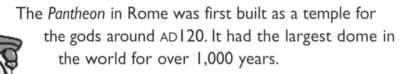

The *Pantheon* in Rome was first built as a temple for the gods around AD120. It had the largest dome in the world for over 1,000 years.

The Roman Colosseum was weather-proof. It had a canvas roof (the *velarium*) that was raised and lowered by a team of Roman sailors.

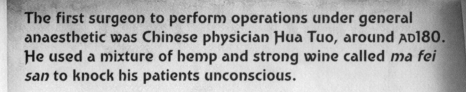

The first surgeon to perform operations under general anaesthetic was Chinese physician Hua Tuo, around AD180. He used a mixture of hemp and strong wine called *ma fei san* to knock his patients unconscious.

The Roman emperor Elagabalus (AD218–222) was so extravagant that he once suffocated some dinner guests to death beneath a mass of sweet-smelling rose petals, which he dropped from the ceiling.

A scary lightning strike in AD228 led the Romans to bury two Greeks and two Celts under the *Forum* (the centre of justice and business in ancient Rome) while they were still alive. It was supposed to stop the gods being angry and sending more lightning.

In the year AD238, six different men reigned as emperor of Rome!

St Lawrence, an early Christian, was martyred in AD258 by being roasted on an outdoor stove. It's said that after a while he called out: 'I am already roasted on one side and, if thou wouldst have me well cooked, it is time to turn me on the other.'

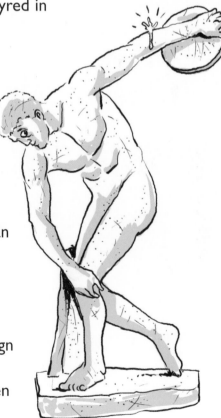

During the reign of Diocletian (AD284–305) it became illegal for a Roman to sell his children as slaves. It's been downhill ever since.

On becoming a gladiator, a man had to sign a contract agreeing to let his employers burn him, chain him up, whip him and even kill him. Not good terms of employment!

The first nation to make Christianity its official religion was Armenia, in AD301.

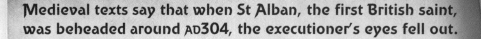

Medieval texts say that when St Alban, the first British saint, was beheaded around AD304, the executioner's eyes fell out.

A Roman cure for epilepsy was to drink the warm blood of a newly killed gladiator.

St Adrian of Nicodemia, who died in AD306, is the patron saint of weapons dealers.

The seven-day week began in AD321. The Roman emperor Constantine chose Sunday as the day of rest to please both the Christians and the pagans.

The most important invention in the history of warfare (prior to gunpowder) was the stirrup, invented in China around AD322. It gave the horse rider greater stability, enabling him to fight more effectively.

Sometimes the Roman Colosseum was flooded with water and was used to stage mock naval battles.

The greatest library in the ancient world was the Library of Alexandria in Egypt. Monks burned it to the ground in AD391. They thought it was a dangerous centre of paganism.

If a Roman owed a lot of people money, they were all allowed to take a sharp knife and cut a slice off him.

A traveller to Britain around AD395 reported that the *Attacotti* tribe were all cannibals who ate the fleshy parts of shepherds and their wives.

In AD406, the Romans were fighting the Vandal army across a wide river. But when the river froze the Vandals simply charged across and beat up the Romans!

Trousers were introduced to the Roman Empire by the Visigoths, who won a battle against Rome in AD410. They soon replaced the traditional toga. Maybe the Romans realized fighting in a skirt put them at a disadvantage – as well as looking silly.

The female scholar Hypatia was murdered in AD415 by a group of crazed monks, who sliced her body into pieces with oyster shells.

One complicated Roman dish involved stuffing a chicken inside a duck, the duck inside a goose, the goose inside a pig, the pig inside a cow, then cooking the whole thing together!

It is said that Attila the Hun (who ruled the Hun kingdom between AD434–453) enjoyed the taste of raw flesh and human blood. Saves on cooking…

It was the custom in ancient Rome for men to place their right hand on their testicles when taking an oath. The modern term 'testimony' is derived from this tradition.

Attila the Hun murdered his wife's brothers. In revenge, she served him the hearts of his two sons (Erp and Eitil) for dinner. What a nice couple…

Bald Romans made a paste from mashed up flies and spread it over their heads to encourage hair growth.

The Romans used to fatten snails to eat. They fed them on salted milk and then plain milk until they were so bloated they couldn't fit back inside their shells. They were then fried and served with a wine sauce.

The fearless warrior Attila the Hun died in AD453 after getting a nosebleed on his wedding night to his new bride.

In AD455, the Vandals sacked Rome with such ferocity that the word *vandalism* came to mean 'senseless destruction'.

St Simeon Stylites of Syria lived alone on top of a pillar for 37 years. He was a popular attraction for many pilgrims and sightseers, even though he just wanted to be alone!

The Romans used to swap actors for convicted criminals in their more gory plays, so they could be tortured and provide entertainment at the same time. At the end of one play, the criminal had to be torn apart by a bear!

If a woman watched even one Olympic event in ancient Greece, she could be executed.

Rome's last emperor, Romulus Augustulus (AD476) shared his first name with the city's legendary founder, Romulus. There's nothing like a neat ending!

A series of gigantic line drawings were created in the Nazca desert in Peru between AD200 and AD700. The Nazca Lines can only be seen from the air and how they were created is a mystery.

A Roman cure for feeling a bit unwell was to eat cabbage for a day, then drink the urine you produced. It probably made you forget the original illness!

The Hideous
Middle Ages

AD478-1499

When a holy person died in the Middle Ages, there would often be a frantic scramble to get a piece of their body – a toe, finger or bone. People kept these parts, called *relics*, as they believed they had special powers like healing illness and protecting people from evil.

In AD493 Theodoric, ruler of the Ostrogoth tribe in eastern Germany defeated Odoacer, king of Italy in battle. After making a toast at a feast celebrating their peace, Theodoric stabbed Odoacer to death.

The Saxons (a group of old Germanic tribes in Europe) had a unique cure for madness – make a whip from the skin of a dolphin, then beat yourself with it. You'd have to be mad to do something as strange as that!

In the Middle Ages people cleaned the leg bones of sheep or pigs, then strapped them to their feet to use as ice skates!

The 'Endless Peace Treaty' signed between Byzantium and Persia in AD533, lasted only seven years. Not exactly endless then!

The Hagia Sophia cathedral in Constantinople was rebuilt for the third time between AD532 and 537. It cost the emperor 145,000 kilograms (320,000 pounds) of gold!

Sometimes Saxon wives were buried alive with their husbands to keep them company in the afterlife. They must have made rather grumpy companions after being buried alive…

The plague of Justinian spread all over the world between AD541 and 542. At its worst it killed between 5,000 and 10,000 people every day. Often, there wasn't enough room to bury the dead, so bodies were left rotting in the streets.

Every silk-producing caterpillar in Europe is descended from two silkworm moth eggs stolen from China and smuggled back to Byzantium (modern-day Istanbul, Turkey).

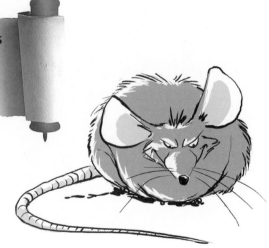

In Saxon England, men were allowed to sell children under seven years old to be slaves 'if they needed to'.

As a Buddhist, Chinese emperor Kao Yang (AD550–559) was not permitted to harm living creatures. When he needed to kill his enemies, he fitted them with bamboo wings and made them try to fly. He killed over 700 rivals in a single year using this method.

Sometimes Saxons cut the heads off their dead relatives before burying them. It was supposed to stop them haunting the living, as without a head they wouldn't be able to find their way back home.

Toilet paper was invented in China in the 6th century AD.

The Loch Ness Monster is first mentioned in the 7th century AD in a book about the life of Saint Columba. It says that in 565 Columba saved a man who was being attacked by a monster in the loch.

During the 7th-century wars between the Welsh and the Saxons, the Welsh took to wearing leeks on the battlefield so that they could spot each other (by smell, at least!). The leek is still the national symbol of Wales.

The most dangerous building project ever was the Grand Canal in China in about AD600. Half of the 5.5 million workers involved died due to the terrible conditions.

The earliest written laws (in a modern language) are those of King Ethelbert of Kent, written in English in AD601.

The religion *Tokoyonomushi* was started in AD644 in Japan. Its devotees worshipped a large worm, got drunk, danced in the streets and gave away all their money.

The only female emperor in China's history was Wu Zetian who ruled between AD690 and 705.

'Greek fire' was a highly effective burning weapon developed by Byzantine Greeks in about AD670. No one now knows how to make it, which is a shame as it sounds impressive – it's said that it burned most fiercely when wet, making it useful in sea battles.

The Battle of Karbala (a city in modern-day Iraq) was possibly the most one-sided conflict of all time. The 40,000-strong army of commander Yazid I faced just 72 followers of commander Husayn ibn Ali. It still took the Yazid army three days to win the battle, in AD680.

When Leontius the Byzantine took control of Eastern Rome in AD695, he had the previous emperor's nose and tongue slit, believing that he would never rule again if he were disfigured. Unluckily for Leontius, Justinian II did return to power in AD705 and paraded Leontius through the streets before killing him.

In AD751, Chinese papermakers were captured by Arabs and forced to reveal their secrets. By AD794, there were state-owned paper mills in Baghdad.

Viking spearsmen claimed to be able to throw two spears at once, hurling one from each hand. They could even catch a spear in flight and throw it back!

The Japanese empress Shotoku, who ruled during the 8th century, had an affair with a Buddhist monk. Their affair was discovered, and after she died, women were forbidden to rule ever again.

Byzantine emperor Constantine VI (reigned AD780–797) met an untimely end. After disfiguring his four uncles for suspected treason, his mother Irene ordered her own soldiers to seize and blind her son. Constantine died from his wounds, leaving Irene in control of his empire.

The term *berserk* means 'bare shirt' in Norse, the Viking language. The Vikings were fearless warriors who went into battle bare-chested – whatever the weather!

The first humans to set foot in Iceland were Irish explorers who arrived there around AD795.

The Vikings would take several ravens on ships with them and would release the birds as they sailed west. The ravens always flew eastwards (towards home) so they could use them to navigate.

King Charlemagne, (ruler of the *Franks* of Central and Western Europe) reigned between AD768 and 814. He refused to allow his seven daughters to marry, as he enjoyed their company so much!

Poor people in Europe used to crush and dry stinging nettles, then weave the fibres into cloth for clothes.

Gunpowder was invented by accident in China during the 9th century AD. The inventor was meant to be creating medicine for a longer life!

During the 800s, the Chinese invented paper armour. Made from multiple layers of folded mulberry paper, it was actually very strong and gave better protection than iron armour, as well as being considerably lighter. The only major drawback was its tendency to catch fire!

King Charlemagne of the Franks died in AD814. His body was mummified and remained seated on the royal throne until 1215 – over 400 years later!

In AD829 the River Nile froze over for the first time in recorded history. It happened again in 1010 but hasn't happened since...

The Chinese invented playing cards in the 9th century. The first card games were played by the women of the emperor's court as a way of passing the time.

Saint Brendan's voyage across the Atlantic Ocean is described in a 9th century manuscript. Its mention of a 'floating crystal castle' may be the first reference to an iceberg.

The world's first printed book was the *Diamond Sutra,* produced in China in AD868. That's 580 years before printing began in Europe.

As Norwegian explorer Ingolfur Arnarson approached Iceland in AD874, he threw two carved pillars overboard, vowing to settle wherever they washed up. The pillars were found on the site of what is now Iceland's capital – Reykjavik.

Inventor Abbas Ibn Firnas achieved the first recorded flight in history. In AD875 he built a glider and launched himself off the top of a mountain near Cordoba, Spain. However, he hadn't worked out how to land and badly injured himself.

Pope Formosus died in AD896. The following year, his rotting corpse was dug up, dressed in his papal robes and put on trial, accused of crimes committed during his life. He was found guilty, had his fingers cut off and was thrown in the river Tiber.

During the 10th century AD, John Overs made a fortune by operating a ferry service across the River Thames near London Bridge, England.

In AD900, Cordoba in Spain had a library of 400,000 books.

Medieval houses in England were made from a framework of wood, with walls made from sticks, mud and either pig or horse manure.

In China in AD910 a relative of the emperor was accidentally killed playing polo. The emperor had the entire opposing team beheaded.

Only one Viking helmet has ever been found – in a Viking grave in southern Norway. It did not have horns, as many people would like to believe!

Fiery, redheaded Viking, Eric the Red (AD950–1003) was exiled from Norway to Iceland for murder. When he got to Iceland, instead of behaving himself, he carried on killing people, was banished even further away and accidentally discovered Greenland!

Abdul Kassam Ismael, ruler of Persia in the 10th century, carried his library with him wherever he went. He travelled with 400 camels carrying his 117,000 books.

Liu Ch'ing, governor of China's Shansi province in AD955, was born with two pupils in each eye.

The first paper money was issued in AD960 in China, as travelling merchants were weighed down by all the coins they had to carry. Europe did not start to use paper currency until 1660.

The worst pope in history was almost certainly John XII. He stole church donations, drank toasts to the devil and prayed to pagan gods when he gambled. In AD964, the husband of a woman he had cheated with beat him to death!

By AD965, there were so many pubs in England that King Edgar decreed there should be no more than one alehouse per village.

A law called *The Truce of God*, written in AD990, banned battles between Wednesday evening and Monday morning and on all holy days. Not that anyone took much notice!

Greenland was given its name to make it attractive to potential settlers. Besides, the name *Iceland* had already been taken...

As the year AD999 drew to a close, people throughout Europe were terrified that the world would end. It's said that Pope Sylvester II's hands were shaking as he gave mass on the last night of the year.

Most places in the world didn't have prisons in the Middle Ages – it was too difficult and expensive to keep people in prison. Instead, punishments were generally death, exile (being kicked out of your homeland) or suffering a horrible mutilation, such as having a bit of your body cut off, pierced or branded.

Before the arrival of mechanical clocks, medieval Europeans divided the day into seven hours of equal length. Because days are longer in summer than in winter, a winter hour was about 60 minutes, but a summer hour was 150 minutes!

It's thought that Pope Sylvester II (AD999–1003) was in fact Jewish and may even have secretly practiced Judaism while he was pope!

In 1014, Byzantine emperor Basil II captured 15,000 Bulgarian prisoners of war. He blinded 99 out of every 100, and gouged out one eye from all the rest. This allowed the ones with a remaining eye to lead the others home. The Bulgarian ruler Samuel died instantly when he saw his blinded army.

Saxon warriors destroyed the original London Bridge, England, in 1014. They rowed their warships up the River Thames, hitched cables around the bridge, then rowed away and pulled it down!

In 1016, King Edmund II of England was using the toilet when he was murdered. An assassin (who had hidden underneath) reached up and stabbed him in the bottom with a long knife. What a dirty job...

In 1020, Sultan Mahmud was so impressed by the beauty of one of the poet Firdausi's rhymes, that he sent a camel loaded with riches to his house. Unfortunately, it arrived on the day of his funeral – bad timing!

In about 1044, the Chinese invented the *excrement bomb*. The bomb was made from a mixture of human faeces, gunpowder and a few nasty chemicals!

The brightest astronomical event in recorded history was the 1054 *supernova* (the explosion of a star). It was so bright that it cast a shadow at night-time!

Mean Englishman John Overs pretended to die, expecting his servants to fast in mourning – saving him the cost of feeding them for a day. Instead, they had a party! When he shouted from his 'deathbed', the servants thought he was a ghost and battered him to death with an oar!

Benedict IV was only around 12 years old when he was made pope in 1032.

On his deathbed, Edward the Confessor pointed to Harold I, which Harold took to mean that he was to be king. Others thought Edward was cursing him, but Harold was handed the English throne anyway!

A medieval punishment for murderers was to have each arm and leg tied to a different horse, then the four horses were made to run in different directions, tearing the criminal apart.

Harold I of England made it an offence for any Welshman to carry a weapon. An armed Welshman would have his hand cut off…which instantly made him an unarmed Welshman!

All knights were right-handed. Left-handed people were thought to be descended from the devil and were banned from becoming knights.

Being king turned out to be a curse for Harold I – he was crowned in 1066 and killed by William the Conqueror the same year.

When William the Conqueror attacked the city of Alençon, France, the people jeered at him for being of lowly birth. When he won the battle, he cut the hands and feet off 32 of the most noble citizens in revenge.

Hereward the Wake, a warrior who fought against the Normans in England, returned from battle to find his brother's head nailed over the door to his family house. That night, he cut the heads off 14 Norman soldiers and nailed their heads over his door instead.

In the late 11th century, William the Conqueror put an end to a rebellion in the north of England by killing every man, boy and farm animal and burning down all the farms.
The remaining people had to eat the dead bodies to survive.

An 11th–century punishment for lying when serving on a jury in court was to have your right hand plunged into a cauldron of boiling water.

After William the Conqueror's death in 1087, his body swelled up with gas as he started to decompose. On the day of his funeral, his stomach exploded, causing a terrible stench. Unable to close the coffin lid, the bishops conducted one of the fastest royal funerals ever recorded.

On his deathbed in 1099, Spanish knight El Cid ordered his men to fasten his corpse to his warhorse after he died, so he could lead them into battle one last time. When the enemy saw the dead man riding towards them, they fled in terror and the Spanish won the battle.

Fishermen in the Fens (a wetland area in eastern England) were still dredging up the skeletons of Norman knights, still in their chain-mail armour 50 years after they had battled with the Saxons.

When the coffin of St Cuthbert was opened 417 years after his death in 687, his body was still fresh and smelled sweet. People thought it was a miracle!

Henry I of England died in 1135 after eating too many *lampreys* (a vicious fish-like an eel), and being treated by a doctor who gave him medicine to cause diarrhoea.

In the 1130s, rebels of the Yanzhou province in China clothed monkeys in straw and set them on fire to cause trouble in the imperial camp.

In 1147 Pope Eugenius III arrived in Paris on a Friday, traditionally a day of fasting. So that the Parisians could celebrate his arrival with a feast, he announced that it was officially Thursday!

During the 1148 siege of Damascus by the *crusaders* (Christian warriors trying to recapture the Holy Land from the Muslims) the wife of a dead Arab archer picked up his bow and took his place. Her arrows struck their standard-bearer and commander, leading to the defeat of the crusaders.

The Order of the Hatchet was an all-female order of knights who successfully fought off an army trying to seize the Spanish town of Tortosa in 1149.

The world's oldest restaurant opened its doors in 1153. *Ma Yu Ching's Bucket Chicken House,* located in Kaifeng, China, has survived wars, invasions and numerous changes of emperor… and is still going to this day!

The Leaning Tower of Pisa began to tilt even before it was completed! Soon after construction began in 1173, the tower began to lean to one side. To compensate for this, the floors were built with one side taller than the other!

Almost every act of a medieval king was public. When emperor Frederick Barbarossa of Germany met with his nobles in 1184, so many of them followed him into the toilet that the floor gave way. The emperor saved himself by grabbing the iron window bars, but many others fell to their death.

Many of the crabs near the coastal town of Danno-ura, Japan, have patterns on their shells that look like the face of a *samurai* warrior (a class of aristocratic Japanese military). Since a samurai defeat in 1185, the fishermen have thrown samurai-pattern crabs back into the sea in shame.

King Henry II of England who reigned from 1154 until his death in 1189, was once whipped by 80 monks. This was his punishment for angry comments he made that led to the murder of Thomas Beckett, the Archbishop of Canterbury. The pair were once close friends.

In 1190 a *troubador* (musical poet) fell in love with a married woman. Her husband sent him away on a crusade where he was killed by a poisoned arrow. He asked his friend to send his heart to his love, but her husband intercepted it, cooked it and fed it to his wife.

During the Third Crusade in 1191, English king Richard the Lionheart ordered his men to throw 100 beehives over the walls of the besieged city of Acre. The terrified people surrendered immediately.

A cowardly soldier who wouldn't fight on a crusade could expect to have his hand pierced right through with a red-hot spike.

A nasty torture device used by the church in the Middle Ages was a metal boot. The victim's foot was fitted into the boot and it was filled with boiling oil.

In 1191, around 2,700 Muslim prisoners were massacred by English king Richard the Lionheart's army to punish Saladin (the ruler of Syria and Egypt) for his non-payment of a ransom. It was one of the great atrocities of the crusades.

King John of England had an effective way of dealing with difficult bishops – he pinned one under a heavy sheet of lead and left him to starve to death.

From the 1200s, the samurai began to dominate Japan. A samurai's two-handed sword, the *katana*, could slice a man in half with a single stroke.

In 1212, a shepherd boy called Nicholas of Cologne led a children's crusade to convert Muslims to Christianity. He led his young followers across the Alps into Italy, but the 7,000 children died of disease and starvation before reaching Jerusalem.

Genghis Khan founded a mighty Mongolian empire in the early 13th century. People were so scared of him, that when his army besieged Beijing in 1215, around 60,000 girls threw themselves to their deaths from the city walls rather than face capture.

Samurai swords were rated for sharpness by how many (dead) human bodies they could slice through in one go. The best swords scored a rating of five bodies.

Around 250 people have fallen off the Leaning Tower of Pisa since it was built.

When Genghis Khan laid siege to one city, he demanded 1,000 cats and 10,000 swallows from the inhabitants. He then tied flaming cloths to their tails and set the animals free, setting fire to the city as they went.

Under medieval law in Europe, animals could be tried and sentenced for crimes. There are records of mice being taken to court for stealing part of the harvest, and a flock of locusts being convicted of eating crops.

Buttons have been used to decorate clothing since at least 2800BC, but it was only in the 13th century AD that someone in Germany thought of using them to fasten clothing.

In 13th-century England, someone who had stolen goods worth more than a shilling (five pence) could have their head chopped off!

When Genghis Khan died in 1227, he was buried beneath a tree near his birthplace. His soldiers killed all witnesses to the funeral (including animals) then killed themselves, so that no living being could know the tomb's location.

The sacrificial knives used by the Aztecs and Incas were made from a black glass called *obsidian* that comes from volcanoes. Obsidian knives are razor-sharp, and never need sharpening.

Genghis Khan's armies always appeared bigger than they really were. Going into battle, each horseman took several spare horses, with dummy soldiers sitting on them. An army of 100,000 soldiers would appear as almost a million!

Relics of saints were so highly valued in the Middle Ages that when holy woman Elisabeth of Thuringia died in 1231, a crowd quickly dismembered her body and stole her bones in anticipation that she would soon be made a saint. She was made a saint, but still, that's no excuse…

Saint Thomas Aquinas was once kidnapped by his own family! When he decided to become a monk in 1244, his family objected and held him captive for over a year. Eventually, Aquinas fled to Paris and became a famous philosopher.

A cure for warts in 1250 was to cut off the head of an eel, rub its blood on the warts and then bury the eel's head. The theory was that as the eel head rotted, the warts would disappear!

People began drilling for oil in the 13th century. Marco Polo saw oil wells on a visit to the Persian city of Baku in 1264.

In 1277, the Chinese invented the first landmines. Buried gunpowder bombs, known as 'underground sky-soaring thunder' were hidden under piles of weapons designed to lure, then kill, passing enemies.

Medieval cities were filthy places! In 1281, it took a gang of men a week to clear 20 tonnes (44,000 pounds) of filth from the cesspit (a dumping ground for human sewage) outside London's Newgate Prison.

Salvino D'Armate of Italy invented the first wearable eyeglasses in 1284. They perched on the bridge of the nose – side arms to hold them on only arrived in the 17th century!

After her coronation in 1286, Queen Margaret, aged 7, suffered terrible seasickness on her journey across the North Sea and died without ever setting foot on the Scottish mainland.

The French were not the first to use the guillotine. From 1286 to 1650 the *Halifax gibbet* operated in Halifax, England. It had a blade that was released by men pulling on a rope. The blade would then drop, decapitating the victim.

In 1287, Mongolian leader Kublai Khan killed a rival by having him wrapped in a carpet and vigorously thrown around. What a way to go!

In 13th century China, anyone whose crops were struck by lightning was excused paying taxes for three years. Lightning was seen as a sign of God's disapproval, so the emperor refused to accept the money in case it was unlucky.

On 26 February 1297, a game was played in the Dutch city of Loenen aan de Vecht involving a stick and leather ball. They called it *kolf*, meaning 'stick' or 'club', so this may have been the first recorded game of golf.

If explorer Marco Polo had not been captured during a war between Venice and Genoa in 1298, we may never have heard of him or his journeys. He told all his stories to a fellow prisoner who persuaded Polo to write them down.

Sir William Wallace, the Scottish rebel leader, had a terrible death after being captured in 1305. He was half-strangled by hanging and was then *disemboweled* (had his intestines cut out!) Finally, he was beheaded and his body was cut into four parts.

In 1314, King Edward II banned football in England for being too violent.

John I of France became king at his birth in 1316, but died five days later.

In 1325, the Italian cities of Bologna and Modena went to war over a stolen bucket.

There are reports of Bibles written on parchment made from human skin in the Middle Ages, but none survive.

In 1347, the plague known as the Black Death reached Europe from Asia. Fleas living on rats spread this deadly disease – if an infected flea bit you you'd catch it and would probably die soon after. It could also be spread through the air by infected peoples' coughs.

People who developed horribly painful *buboes* (swellings) were the lucky plague victims – they had a small chance of recovering. The unlucky ones died before any buboes formed, sometimes in a few minutes.

Oxford University, England, once had a rule forbidding students to bring bows and arrows into class.

During a typical medieval siege, missiles thrown by catapults occasionally included rotten food, dead horses and even captured soldiers.

In European *zoology* (animal) books in the Middle Ages, dragons were listed as real animals!

In 1347, a Mongolian army used a catapult to launch plague victims into the enemy city of Caffa. They hoped the citizens would catch the plague and be easier to defeat. It was a pretty gruesome weapon!

The Black Death spread from Asia to Europe, but killed very few Mongolian *nomads* (people with no fixed home) because they spent a lot of time with horses – the fleas that carried the plague hated the smell of horses!

Some favourite medieval pastimes in England were bear-baiting, bull-baiting, cock-fighting or horse-fighting. People would poke the animals with sharp sticks or set dogs on them to make them fight. People betted on the animal they wanted to win.

The Incas did not have iron, but they had so much gold that they used it for everyday objects such as nails, eating utensils, combs and eyebrow tweezers!

During the Black Death, a law was passed requiring people to say 'God bless you' when they heard someone sneeze!

Perfumes made from flowers, oils and spices were very popular during the Middle Ages. Perfume became an easy solution for people who could not bathe.

The Black Death lasted three years, killing 25 million people – a third of the European population.

In the Middle Ages, people used shark skin as sandpaper because it's covered in tiny teeth called denticles.

A plague of drunkenness spread through many European towns in the mid 14th century. Many people thought that alcohol would protect them against the Black Death. It didn't.

In 1348, over a million pilgrims held a mass prayer meeting in Rome to combat the plague. Sadly, it spread rapidly through the crowd and fewer than ten per cent of the pilgrims lived to return home.

When the mistress of Prince Pedro of Portugal, Inés de Castro, was murdered in 1355, he had her body preserved. When he became king, he had her exhumed and placed on a throne beside him at the coronation feast. Nobles and clergy had to kiss the corpse's hand.

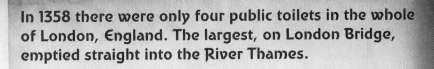

In 1358 there were only four public toilets in the whole of London, England. The largest, on London Bridge, emptied straight into the River Thames.

The plague would kill you instantly if a poisonous flea bite got straight into your bloodstream. That form of the disease killed between 95 and 100 per cent of people who caught it.

When the Mongol conqueror, Tamerlane, besieged the city of Sivas in Turkey, he promised not to spill a drop of the residents' blood if they surrendered. The citizens agreed and he kept his word – sort of…4,000 Armenians were burned alive, all the Christians were strangled or drowned and others were trampled to death. The Turks were safe though, as Tamerlane had Turkish relatives!

Hung Wu, the first emperor of the Ming dynasty in China, was so fearful of the rebellious city of Peiping, that in 1368 he ordered the entire city to be destroyed.

Between 1370 and 1405, the Mongol leader Tamerlane ordered a tower to be constructed using live men, heaped on top of one another and cemented together with bricks and mortar.

Chinese emperor Hung Wu's harshness was legendary. He had so many people executed that it became customary for government officials to say their last goodbyes to their families if they were summoned for a meeting with him!

King Richard II who reigned over England between 1377 and 1399, sometimes gave feasts for as many as 10,000 people at once! Records show that one of these parties required 140 hogs, 14 oxen, 12 calves and 12 boars.

The world's oldest treaty of alliance still in operation is the Treaty of Windsor signed by England and Potugal in 1386. It's an agreement of mutual support between the two countries.

In 1393, records state that the Chinese Bureau of Imperial Supplies manufactured 720,000 sheets of toilet paper for the entire court. A further 15,000 yellow-tinted, perfumed sheets were made exclusively for the use of the emperor and his family.

A scholar who was angry with emperor Hung Wu's policies decided to confront the emperor. He brought his own coffin with him and after delivering his speech he climbed into the coffin, expecting the emperor to execute him on the spot. Hung Wu was so impressed with the man's bravery that he spared his life.

In the 1400s, the Incas of South America built a huge empire stretching through modern Peru and Chile. They controlled the empire by building 30,000 kilometres (18,639 miles) of paved roads and even suspension bridges across the ravines!

In most European cities in the Middle Ages, a drainage channel ran down the middle of the street and all kinds of sloppy rubbish would be thrown into it: the contents of chamber pots and lavatories; the innards from animals slaughtered for meat and anything else yukky that was lying around!

In 1425, when she was 17 years old, Joan of Arc led the defence of Orleans in France, freeing the city in just nine days. She was captured by the English two years later and burned at the stake as a witch because she claimed the voices of saints had directed her.

Many people in Europe believed the Black Death was spread by 'bad air' and thought they could protect themselves by inhaling strong smells. Some sniffed bunches of fragrant herbs but others crouched for hours over cess-pits, breathing in the stench. Rotten!

It was illegal for women to wear buttons in 15th-century Florence.

Despite the vastness of their empire, the Incas had an effective communications network. By the use of relay runners stationed every 2.5 kilometres (1.5 miles) a message could travel 250 kilometres (155 miles) in less than a day!

Potatoes, pumpkins and pineapples were all grown first by the Incas of South America.

The English conquered Ireland in the 12th century, but by the 1400s they controlled only a small area around Dublin called 'The Pale'. The phrase 'beyond the pale' is taken from the wild and unconquered places in Ireland outside English rule.

A group known as *flagellants* believed the Black Death was a punishment from God. As penance for their sins, they went from town to town, chanting hymns and whipping themselves with metal-studded straps.

To punish a revolt in Persia, Mongol leader Tamerlane had the entire population massacred. He left behind a pyramid of 70,000 skulls piled up outside the city walls.

In 1410, the Dutch painter Jan van Eyck popularized oil painting. He used a mixture of glass, bones and mineral pigments boiled in linseed oil to make his paint.

Italian engineer Giovanni di Fontana designed a rocket car in 1425. The rocket was powered by a secret fuel consisting mainly of gunpowder. If it had ever been built, it would certainly have exploded on take off...

Vlad the Impaler ruled *Wallachia* (present-day Romania) from 1456 to 1462. When 55 Turkish ambassadors refused to remove their hats in his presence he had their hats nailed to their heads.

In 1471, a court in Switzerland sentenced a chicken to death for laying a brightly coloured egg!

The Spanish Inquisition was formed in 1481 and officially operated until 1834 to enforce the laws of the Catholic Church and get rid of heretics (those opposed to the views of the church), Jews and Muslims. The Inquisition executed thousands of people and tortured many more.

Tattooing criminals with symbols that marked them out as outcasts was a common punishment in medieval Japan. In one region, all criminals had the symbol for a dog tattooed on their foreheads.

The Italian philosopher Marsilio Ficino (1433–1499) recorded that some people would sell elderly people their blood. The old patients sucked it directly from the seller's veins, as medicine.

In the Aztec festival of *Tlacaxipehualiztli* or 'the flaying of men' a sacrificial victim was skinned alive and then a warrior would dress in the skin.

Women during the Middle Ages would only wear their hair loose on their wedding night.

Tortures used by the Spanish Inquisition included the *garrucha*, in which the accused was suspended from the ceiling by a pulley with weights tied to the ankles, often dislocating their arms and legs.

In 1487 the Aztecs of central Mexico sacrificed 20,000 people in four days. The queues of victims, in four lines, were over 3 kilometres (1.8 miles) long.

Those found guilty of heresy by the Spanish Inquisition may be burned at the stake. Around 2,000 people were executed between 1481 and 1490.

An early attempt at a blood transfusion took place in 1492 to try and save the life of Pope Innocent VIII. The blood of three boys was given to him through his mouth. They didn't know much about blood circulation at the time – the pope died and so did the three boys.

Mongol leader Tamerlane played polo with the skulls of people he had killed in battle.

In 1492, Christopher Columbus left Spain in search of a western route to India. Instead he became the first European to set foot in America. Unaware of his mistake, he called the native people Indians. He died in 1502, without knowing he hadn't found India!

The Aztecs believed the tears of children would make the rains come and improve their harvest. They trapped children in mountain caves to make them cry, and sometimes let them starve to death.

In 1493, the Italian artist and scientist Leonardo da Vinci drew sketches of a flying machine that look surprisingly like a modern helicopter.

The stepped Aztec pyramids on which human sacrifices took place had channels for the blood to run down, right next to the stairs.

The toothbrush was invented in China in 1498. The handles were made from bamboo and the bristles were the stiff, coarse hairs taken from the back of a hog's neck.

Leonardo da Vinci was centuries ahead of his time with many of his ideas, which included sketches for bicycles, submarines, mechanical saws, contact lenses, scissors and tanks!

The first known white wedding dress was worn by Anne of Brittany in 1499. It was an unusual choice – at the time, white was the colour of mourning.

Leonardo da Vinci produced one of the first textbooks on human anatomy. He cut up the corpses of executed criminals and sketched what he saw. He also found time to do a spot of painting…among his works was the *Mona Lisa*, the most famous painting of all time!

The Hideous
Dawn of Discovery

1500-1699

Brides first carried bouquets of flowers in the 16th century to cover up their nasty body odour!

A 16th-century cure for *jaundice* (a liver disease) was to drink a beer containing nine head lice, each morning. It may not have cured the jaundice but they must have got rid of all their head lice!

The Tudor family held the throne in England between 1485 and 1603. It was a period of fights and rebellion. Criminals faced harsh punishments such as being hanged, burned alive, whipped, branded with a hot iron or being chained up and pelted with rotten food!

In 1502, the Italian explorer Christopher Columbus was the first European to taste chocolate.

Tudor King Henry VIII reigned over England from 1509 until his death and married six times. The lucky ones escaped with divorce – two had their heads chopped off!

King Francis I of France who ruled between 1515 and 1547 always travelled with a small piece of an ancient Egyptian mummy! He used it as a medicine to soothe bruises.

When the Spanish *conquistador* (conqueror) Hernan Cortes landed in Mexico in 1518, the native Aztecs thought he was a God!

To help babies with the pain of teething, a Tudor mum might rub a dead hare on the baby's gums.

In Tudor England, many women wore a lead-based white make-up that literally ate away their skin. They also put poisonous juices from the deadly nightshade plant into their eyes to make their pupils bigger. They must have looked lovely...

Henry VIII carried his own portable toilet with him wherever he went. The 'royal stool' was a large box with a feather-padded seat on the lid and a potty inside.

A Tudor cure for *gout* (a painful illness affecting the joints) was to boil a red-haired dog in oil, mix in some worms, pig marrow and herbs and then spread the smelly mixture wherever it hurt!

Under the reign of Henry VIII, around 70,000 people were executed. That's a lot of heads rolling on the floor!

In the 1500s, an entire family would use the same bathwater. The baby would go in last of all, when it was really dirty!

European executioners in the 16th and 17th centuries often wore grotesque iron masks that made them look scary – as if being executed wasn't scary enough already!

Tudor people believed that if they wore fur, any fleas would jump off them and on to the fur instead!

Ferdinand Magellan is often considered the first man to have sailed round the world, but in fact he died on the voyage in 1521 and his officer Juan Sebastian del Cano finished the expedition for him.

In 1531, Richard Roose, chef to the Bishop of Rochester, was sentenced to death for poisoning members of the bishop's household. He was dropped into a pot of water hanging over a fire in the town square. It took two hours for the water to boil and kill him.

The Spanish conquistador Francisco Pizarro conquered the mighty Inca Empire in 1532 with just 180 men, one cannon and 27 horses.

Henry VIII's second wife, Anne Boleyn was believed to have had eleven fingers and three breasts.

Ivan the Terrible became the first *tsar* (king) of Russia in 1547. He was poisoned and killed while playing a game of chess in 1584.

The bodies of sacrificial victims in 16th-century central Mexico were fed to the snakes that guarded the holy Aztec temples.

Following his execution in 1535, English statesman, scholar and lawyer, Sir Thomas More's head was stuck on a pole at London Bridge. More's daughter paid the bridge keeper to knock it down. She caught it, took it home and kept it. Then, when she died, she was buried with it.

A Tudor cure for asthma was the lungs of a fox mixed with wine and liquorice.

When Anne Boleyn was beheaded in 1536 on grounds of treason, there was no coffin provided for her. Her body was stuck in an old arrow chest with the head tucked beneath the arm.

In 1540, Henry VIII got engaged to Anne of Cleves without even meeting her. When he saw her, he found her very ugly, but he didn't change his mind – five months after their wedding, he had the marriage cancelled.

In 1541, the Franciscan monk Diego de Landa burned all the books of the South American Maya people. But he was sorry – he spent his final days asking Mayan survivors to tell him their history, and tried to recreate what he had destroyed.

Mary Queen of Scots who reigned in Scotland between 1542 and 1567, kept a 'unicorn's horn' with her throughout her 19-year imprisonment in England, dipping it into her food to test for poison. The 'unicorn horn' was really the horn of a *narwhal*, a sea mammal with a long tusk.

The night before Henry VIII's fifth wife, Catherine Howard was executed in 1542, she asked for the chopping block to be brought to her cell in the Tower of London. She spent the night practising putting her head on the block so there would be a clean cut on the first try.

Ivan the Terrible beat his own son to death in a fit of rage.

When he died in 1547, Henry VIII weighed over 182 kilograms (400 pounds). He was constantly breathless and purple in the face. Ulcers on his swollen legs had to be dressed several times a day and gave off a terrible smell.

Mary I of England, known as 'Bloody Mary' executed more than 200 Protestants when she reigned over England between 1553 and 1558.

In Tudor England, *chilblains* (itchy, painful lumps on the skin) were treated by covering them with the hot skin of a mouse!

Lady Jane Grey (the Queen of England for just nine days in 1533) was beheaded along with her husband and father in 1554, once the throne had passed to 'Bloody Mary'. Her father's mummified head is still on display in the church of St Botolph Aldgate in London.

The famous French visionary, Nostradamus is said to have predicted the Great Fire of London, the French Revolution, the rise of Napoleon Bonaparte and Adolf Hitler, and both World Wars – all in 1555!

The first known victim of the torture device 'the rack' was Cuthbert Simpson, who was tortured for being a Protestant during the reign of Bloody Mary. His hands and feet were tied to rollers and turned opposite ways until his joints popped and he died.

Life expectancy in Tudor England was just 35 years.

The worst earthquake in history occurred in 1556 in China's Shansi Province, killing 830,000 people.

After 'Bloody Mary' came Elizabeth I who reigned over England for 45 years between 1558 and 1603, when she died of blood poisoning.

When Ivan the Terrible found out his sixth wife was having an affair, he had her boyfriend impaled on a spike and left to die outside her bedroom window.

Elizabeth I almost died of smallpox in 1562. She survived, but was left with big scars on her face, so she wore thick, lead-based make up to cover them up.

In 1565, an enormous graphite deposit was found in Cumbria, England. Locals found it useful for marking sheep and the humble pencil was born soon after!

The first potato to arrive in Europe was the *tetraploid Andean short day potato,* which arrived in southern Spain in about 1565. Quite a mouthful!

Many Catholic houses in England contained 'priest holes' – concealed rooms where priests could hide during the persecution of Catholics in the reign of Elizabeth I.

One event that Nostradamus predicted with absolute certainty was his own death. 'You will not find me alive at sunrise' he told his secretary on 1 July 1566. He was discovered dead the next morning.

When the Earl of Oxford, Edward de Vere, accidentally passed wind while bowing before Queen Elizabeth I, he was so embarrassed that he left court for seven years. On his return, Elizabeth greeted him by saying: 'My Lord, I had forgot the fart'!

After a dispute with the city of Novgorod in 1570, Ivan the Terrible ordered the torture and death of every citizen. Many had their fingernails, tongues, hands, ears or ribs torn out with red-hot pincers.

Artists in the 16th century sometimes added powdered Egyptian mummy to their paint! They believed it would stop the surface from cracking when it was dry.

In England in 1571, a man could be fined for not wearing a woollen cap.

On 24 August 1572, 70,000 Huguenots (French Protestants) were killed on the orders of the Catholic queen Catherine de Medici.

Ivan the Terrible's marriage to his seventh wife lasted just one day. Discovering she already had a boyfriend, he had his new bride drowned.

For 15 years from 1575, Persian poet Abu'l-Fazl ibn Mubarak was the personal tutor to the three sons of emperor Akbar in India. Each year he was paid the combined weight of his three students in gold.

The Innuit practice of tattooing was first recorded in 1576 (but had been going on since 1500BC). Tattoo artists were women, who stitched the tattoo into the skin with a stain made with soot, graphite and urine.

In the 1580s, Sir Walter Raleigh was one of the first Europeans to bring tobacco from the New World (America). While Raleigh was enjoying a pipe one day, his servant threw a pot of water over his head to put out the fire!

In 1582, Pope Gregory XIII decreed that ten whole days should be skipped – people going to bed on 4 October woke up on 15 October. There were riots, as people argued that their lives had been shortened!

The question mark was invented in the 1580s.

When Mary Queen of Scots was executed in 1587 it took three blows of the executioner's axe to remove her head completely.

On being told of the approach of the Spanish Armada (fleet of war ships) in 1588, Sir Francis Drake insisted on finishing his game of bowls. He won the battle – it's not recorded whether he won at bowls!

Plague outbreaks were common around Europe in the 16th and 17th centuries. One 'cure' that people tried was to hold a cockerel's bottom on a plague sore for as long as possible. If the cockerel died, you had to get another, split it in half while still alive and put that on the sore. This was very economical (two people could be treated with the second cockerel!) but sadly never worked...

The Duke of Medina, who led the Spanish Armada against England in 1588, hated the sea and suffered from terrible seasickness. Unfortunate considering his line of work!

Sawney Bean, his wife, eight sons and 32 grandchildren lived in a cave in Scotland in the late 16th century. Over a 25-year period, they kidnapped more than 1,000 local people and took them back to their cave where they cut them up and ate them.

When the Egyptian government stopped the export of mummies in the late 16th century, locals set up mummy factories that mummified people who had recently died, and sold them instead!

When King James VI of Scotland learned of the cannibal Bean family, he sent 400 men with dogs to hunt them down. They were captured and taken in chains to Edinburgh where they were executed without trial.

In 1588, the British mathematician and innkeeper William Bourne designed a submarine. It had a wooden frame covered with waterproofed leather and was rowed like a boat.

The victory of a war between Burma and Thailand in 1591 was decided by single combat between the two rival kings, each riding an elephant.

In 1596, Englishman Sir John Harrington invented the first flushing toilet. Queen Elizabeth I was so impressed with it that she had one built at Richmond Palace.

Crimes that carried the death penalty in Elizabethan England included letting the water out of ponds and stealing hawks.

The Globe Theatre, which opened on London's South Bank in 1599, was built using the materials from an earlier playhouse called The Theatre. The owners of The Theatre transported the timber across the River Thames and reconstructed it as the Globe. Who said they weren't good at recycling?!

Akbar the Great, who ruled Mughal India between 1556 and 1605, died in 1605 after being poisoned by his own family.

King James I of England, who reigned between 1603 and 1625, was the first English monarch to have more than one name (Charles James Stuart).

In 1584, Dmitri Ivanovic, the three-year-old heir to the Russian throne, was murdered. Then in 1604, a man calling himself Dmitri Ivanovic, claimed he had miraculously survived the assassination. He invaded Russia and crowned himself tsar. He was actually a monk called Gregory Otrepiev!

The handwriting on Guy Fawkes' two signed confessions is so different, that he was probably tortured on the rack, damaging his arm muscles. He had tried to blow up James I and the Houses of Parliament on 5th November, 1605.

Elizabeth Bathory was a sadistic Hungarian countess who liked to torture young women in the early 1600s. One of her entertainments was to place them in her courtyard on a freezing night and pour water over them to turn them into 'ice statues'.

Two of the most notorious pirates of the 17th century were women – Mary Read and Anne Bonny.

Guy Fawkes was sentenced to be hanged, drawn (dragged along the ground) and quartered (cut into four pieces) for his involvement in the Gunpowder Plot, but he escaped this grisly execution by jumping off the scaffold and breaking his neck instead.

The Christmas decoration industry received a boost in 1610 with the German invention of tinsel. It was quite a luxury at the time, as they used real silver!

The favourite weapon of Murad IV (sultan of the Ottoman Empire 1612–1640) was a huge club covered in metal spikes. It weighed 60 kilograms (132 pounds) and he could swing it easily with just one hand!

On 29 June 1613, London's Globe Theatre burned down when a spark from a theatrical cannon caused a fire during a performance of Shakespeare's *Henry VIII*.

In the early 17th century, Holland became gripped by a mania for tulip bulbs. A type of tulip infected with a virus that produced a pattern of multi-coloured stripes on the petals was the most popular!

Shakespeare (c.1564–1616) used about 29,000 words in his plays, 10,000 of which had never previously been used in any English literary work.

Following his execution in 1618, Sir Walter Raleigh's wife kept his embalmed head in a red leather bag for 29 years. She even carried it around with her until it got too smelly...

Sultan Murad IV banned coffee and coffeehouses after overhearing some people in a coffeehouse criticizing his leadership. Murad later died of alcohol poisoning – perhaps he banned the wrong drink...

English philosopher Sir Francis Bacon invented frozen food during a snowstorm in 1625, when he killed a chicken and tried to stuff it with snow! Bacon died of pneumonia in 1626 as a result of messing around in the snow.

Many European cities started to publish 'bills of mortality' from the 15th century onwards. The bills listed all deaths in the city, and often the causes of death. Entries for London in 1629 include 'planet struck', 'worms', 'excessive drinking' and 'suddenly'!

King Charles II of England (1630–85) used to rub himself all over with dust made from powdered Egyptian mummies in the belief that the greatness of the pharaohs would rub off on him.

Queen Christina of Sweden who ruled between 1632 and 1689, so detested the fleas that infested her bedchamber that she had a miniature, 10 centimetre (4 inch) cannon built so she could fire tiny cannonballs at them!

The English dramatist Ben Jonson died in 1637. He was buried standing up in Westminster Abbey.

In 17th-century Europe, 'corpse medicine' was very popular. This was medicine made from parts of dead bodies.

The typical American log cabin is not really an American invention. Swedish settlers who moved to Delaware in 1638 brought the design with them.

The last English monarch to enter the Chamber of the House of Commons was King Charles I in 1642, who went there to arrest five MPs on a charge of treason.

Galileo (1564–1642) was not only an astronomer, but also an inventor. His inventions ranged from a basic thermometer to an automatic tomato-picking machine!

19-year-old Blaise Pascal of Rouen, France invented the first digital adding-up machine in 1644. The machine could add and subtract numbers up to eight digits long. He invented it to help his father with his sums.

King Charles I of England had a lucky black cat that he guarded day and night. The cat died in February 1647 and the very next day Charles was arrested and handed over to his enemies, eventually to be beheaded…

In the 17th century, a Dutch sailor was thrown into prison for mistaking a tulip bulb for an onion and eating it. Tulips were much loved!

On the morning of his execution in January 1649, King Charles I of England put on two shirts. It was a cold day and he didn't want witnesses to think that he was shivering from fear.

A 1649 American law in Massachusetts declared that the punishment for stubbornness was death.

Soon after the Taj Mahal's completion in 1653, Mughal emperor Shah Jahan fell ill and was imprisoned by his son in a nearby fort. He spent the rest of his life gazing through the window at the Taj Mahal, which he had built as a tomb for his late wife.

In 1654, Irish Archbishop James Ussher announced the precise date and time of creation. He calculated that it took place on Sunday, 21 October 4004BC at 9 o'clock in the morning!

In December of 1657, the Massachusetts General Court in America ordered that anyone celebrating Christmas would be fined.

On the 26th March 1658, the famous London diarist Samuel Pepys (1633–1703) had a bladder stone the size of a tennis ball removed without any anaesthetic – four strong men had to hold him down! Every year on the anniversary of this operation, Pepys toasted his kidney stone (kept in a bottle at home) with a glass of wine.

Between 1500 and 1650, Spanish *conquistadors* (conquerors) shipped 180 tonnes (400,000 pounds) of gold and 16,000 tonnes (3.5 million pounds) of silver from the Americas back to Europe!

When Oliver Cromwell, Lord Protector of England died in 1658 his body was embalmed. Two years later it was dug up and displayed in a *gibbet* (a sort of metal cage), then his head was cut off and put on a spike for 24 years in London. Eventually it fell off and was stolen by a soldier who kept it in his chimney!

A special type of moss that grows on human skulls was a popular medicine for nosebleeds in the 17th century. To avoid being defrauded by people selling any old moss, rich people would buy an entire skull with the 'skull moss' still in place.

In 1658, the Paris police raided a monastery and arrested 12 monks for eating meat and drinking wine during Lent.

Tea became fashionable in England in 1662 when King Charles II started drinking it.

Oliver Cromwell's embalmed head is now hidden in a secret location in Sidney Sussex College, Cambridge. Only two people at any time know where it is – when one dies, another person is told...

King Charles II of England, who reigned between 1660 and 1685, was a strong supporter of 'corpse medicine'. He made a distillation from a human skull in his own laboratory, and was dependent on it during his final illness. The fact that it was his final illness before he died suggests it didn't work very well...

In 1665, the Great Plague broke out in London, killing 80,000 people.

In 1666 a terrible fire destroyed 80 per cent of London, but the death toll was very low – perhaps only about ten people.

The first successful blood transfusion took place on 15 June 1667 when the blood of a sheep was transfused into a teenage boy. The boy survived, but there is no record of what happened to the sheep...

In 1670, highwayman Claude Duval held up a coach containing a nobleman and his wife. To prove she wasn't afraid, the lady played a tune on her pipe and did a dance. Duval asked her husband for £400 ($798) of which he kept £100 ($199) for himself – he gave the rest back to the lady for the pleasure of her dance!

On 9 May 1671, Thomas Blood and his gang were caught trying to steal the Crown Jewels from the Tower of London. Blood refused to speak to anyone but the king, Charles II. No one knows what he said, but Blood was released from his cell and given an annual pension of £500 ($998)!

Peter the Great (1672–1725) was the 'greatest' of all the Russian tsars, in more ways than one – he was well over 2 metres (6 feet 5 inches) tall!

One of the first references to ice cream in Western Europe came in 1672 when it was served to King Charles II of England.

In 1673, Dutch scientist Anthony van Leeuwenhoek developed an early microscope and was the first person to see micro-organisms.

Once, in 17th-century Holland, an entire house was traded for a single tulip bulb.

During the execution of a Native American Indian in Massachusetts in 1675, a friend of the victim rushed forward, cut a hole in the victim's chest and sucked out his blood. When questioned, he said that it would give him the strength of two men.

The world's oldest public museum is the Ashmolean Museum in Oxford, England, which opened its doors in 1683.

In 1685, due to a shortage of coins, the North American colony of New France used playing cards as currency.

Paskah Rose was appointed royal executioner to King James II of England in 1686. He'd only been in the job a few months when he himself was hanged for the theft of a coat!

The French composer and conductor Jean-Baptiste Lully used a very large baton which he pounded on the floor in time to the music. At a concert in 1687, Lully accidentally stuck the staff into his foot. He developed gangrene and died that year.

Edward Russell, Earl of Orton, was known for his extravagant lifestyle. At a party in the 1690s, he used his garden fountain as a giant punch bowl. The bartender rowed about on a small boat, filling up the cups!

In 1697, the young Russian tsar, Peter the Great secretly travelled to Europe. He and his companions behaved like rock stars, drinking to excess and trashing hotel rooms!

The Hideous
Revolutionary Years

1700-1849

In 1705, the Russian emperor Peter the Great passed a law making beards illegal. Anyone who grew a beard was fined!

The most notorious pirate was Edward Teach (1680–1718), known as *Blackbeard*. He would leap into action with exploding firecrackers tied to his bushy black beard.

The most famous English highwayman, Dick Turpin (1706–1739), originally had a partner called Tom King. The partnership ended when Turpin accidentally shot him.

In the early 1700s, a cook in Belgium started deep-frying chips of potato. Thomas Jefferson introduced the idea to the Americans in the 1790s, describing them as 'potatoes, fried in the French manner'. The term 'French fries' annoys some Belgians to this day!

The French king, Louis XIV, requested that his heart be embalmed after his death. In 1715, he died and his heart was mummified. It was stolen during the French Revolution and is rumoured to have been eaten by English geologist William Buckland in the 19th century!

In the 18th century, doctors were becoming more interested in how the human body worked – but they needed to cut up dead bodies to find out more. It was illegal to dissect dead people, so they had to pay grave robbers to steal newly-buried bodies, or take hanged criminals from the gallows.

The pirate Blackbeard once shot one of his crew in the knee for no apparent reason, leaving him crippled for life. He did it to scare his fellow pirates.

The machine gun was invented in 1718 by Englishman James Puckle. The Puckle gun could fire nine shots per minute while a standard musket could fire only three.

In the early 1700s, England fell victim to the 'gin craze'. There were more than 7,500 gin shops in London.

An 18th-century vaccination against smallpox was made by taking pus from the sores on a dairymaid's hands and rubbing it onto a scratch on the patient's arm.

The infamous pirate Blackbeard had a vast hoard of treasure buried somewhere secret. His crew begged him to tell them where it was (in case he died) but he took his secret to the grave when he died in 1718.

The 18th century was the 'golden age' of highwaymen. Many were of gentlemanly birth and to be robbed by one was almost regarded as an honour!

Executioners earned extra money by cutting the head from hanging victims, cleaning it of flesh, brains and other bloody-bits and then selling it for medicine.

In 18th-century England, people who had committed suicide were buried at a crossroads with a stake through their hearts. The crossroads were supposed to confuse a ghost so that it couldn't find its way home and the stake was to keep the body in the ground!

Blackbeard met his end on 21 November 1718 when Robert Maynard of the British Navy was sent to capture him. Blackbeard jumped aboard Maynard's ship, where he received five gunshot wounds and at least 20 sword wounds before he fell down, dead.

James MacLaine (1724–1750) was known as 'the gentleman highwayman' because he was very polite to his victims. He accidentally shot the writer Horace Walpole during a hold-up, so he sent him a letter of apology the next day. If only all criminals were that well mannered!

In 1726, Englishwoman Mary Toft claimed she had given birth to five rabbits. In fact, her husband had been slipping her the rabbits when no one was looking so that she could 'produce' them at the appropriate moment. What a strange trick!

Mathematician and physicist, Sir Isaac Newton's only recorded speech while he was a Member of Parliament was a request to open the window! He died in 1727, aged 84.

A common pirate punishment was *keelhauling*. Victims were tied to a rope and dragged under the ship, then up the other side. They emerged half drowned, with their skin shredded by the barnacles that grew on the ship's hull.

Dick Turpin's career as a violent, highway robber ended when he was arrested for shooting his landlord's rooster. A former schoolmaster recognized him while he was awaiting trial and he was hanged in York, England, in 1739.

The War of Jenkins' Ear between England and Spain erupted in 1739, after the Spanish cut off the ear of Captain Robert Jenkins. It was a warning to English traders to keep away from their American colonies.

In 1740, a French cow was found guilty of sorcery and hanged.

In 1741, Arctic explorers found that the local people decorated their bodies with piercings threaded with bones. They wore them through their chin, forehead or nose.

In 1743 King Louis XV of France installed the world's first indoor elevator in his palace, calling it his 'flying chair'.

Roller skates made their debut on a London stage in 1743.

Highwayman James MacLaine's luck ran out when he tried to sell the coat of one of his victims, Lord Elgington. The coat was recognized and MacLaine was caught. He was hanged in 1750.

Francis Henry Egerton (1756–1829) the Eighth Earl of Bridgewater, gave dinner parties for dogs, dressing them in the latest fashions of the day – including fancy miniature shoes!

In 1758, British settlers tried to infect Native American tribes by giving them blankets from dead smallpox patients.

The composer Wolfgang Amadeus Mozart (1756–1791) was a competent musician by the age of four and wrote his first compositions aged five!

The high, elaborate wigs worn in Europe from 1760 onwards were often filled with vermin – so people carried special jeweled sticks to poke them out.

The pirate flag (a black skull and crossbones) was known as the *Jolly Roger*. It was not feared as much as the red flag, which meant that no mercy would be shown to victims.

On 25 October 1760, King George II became the second English king to die on the toilet.

The tune for the American national anthem, *The Star-Spangled Banner*, was composed around 1765 by an Englishman called John Stafford Smith as a drinking song.

To protect their dead relatives from being stolen by bodysnatchers, many people would take it in turn to grave-watch for a couple of weeks until the body was too rotten to steal.

Eccentric Englishwoman Hannah Beswick was terrified of being buried alive. Before her death in 1768, she promised her doctor a large inheritance if he preserved her body for 100 years and regularly checked to see if she was alive.

Napoleon's real name was Italian: Napoleone di Buonaparte. He was born in Corsica in 1769, one year after the island was purchased by the French – so he was only just French!

An Englishman called William Addis invented the first mass-produced toothbrush while he was serving time in prison, around 1770.

William Carlisle of Rhode Island, USA, was convicted of forgery in 1771. He was sentenced to have both ears cut off and to be branded with the letter 'R' for 'rogue' on both cheeks.

Number 10 Downing Street, residence of the British Prime Minister, was completed in 1772. The door can only be opened from the inside!

Thomas Jefferson, third president of the USA, designed his own home in 1772. It included automatic doors, the first swivel chair and a machine to copy letters – all invented by him!

In 1773, American colonists disguised as Mohawk Indians invaded a merchant ship in Boston and threw its cargo of tea into the sea. It was a protest against the taxes on tea imposed by the British and is known as 'The Boston Tea Party'.

The Highway Act of 1773 recommended that horse traffic should keep to the left. British drivers have remained on the left ever since!

When Captain Cook arrived in Hawaii in 1779, he allowed the natives to worship him as their god. After he sailed away, a storm forced him back to the island. The natives were shocked. How could a god fall victim to the elements? Feeling betrayed, they beat him to death.

Rich people would pay the equivalent of many thousands of pounds to rent a house opposite the gallows outside Newgate prison in London, England, to watch a famous criminal hang.

In December 1783, Louis-Sébastien Lenormand jumped from the top of the Montpelier Observatory in France with a parachute, landing unharmed. He had designed it as a kind of portable fire escape.

Napoleon always carried chocolate with him on his military campaigns and ate some before battles for an energy boost!

The dollar sign was adopted to signify the US currency in 1785. It probably comes from the Spanish coat of arms, which shows the two *Pillars of Hercules* with an S-shaped ribbon running through them.

The Sumptuary Laws of 18th-century Japan restricted which colours people could wear. Only the imperial family could wear yellow, and blue was reserved for the nobility

The first parachute jump from an aircraft was made by a dog! It was dropped from a hot air balloon by Frenchman Jean-Pierre Blanchard in 1785.

In 1786, Frenchwoman Marie-Augustin was sent to prison for 50 years for whistling at Queen Marie Antoinette as she was entering a theatre.

In 1789, hanging, rather than burning, became the official method of execution in Britain.

The last woman to be executed by burning in Britain was Catherine Murphy in 1789. She was convicted of making counterfeit coins.

Shoelaces were invented in England on 27 March 1790.

In the 18th century, ladies used 'the language of the fan' – gestures made with the fan to send messages and flirt silently. In Spain, around 60 fan phrases developed.

When Mozart died in 1791, he had only one pallbearer and his coffin was buried in an unmarked pauper's grave.

On 21 June 1791, the French royal family tried to escape from the Tuileries Palace in Paris, where they were held captive. All went well until Louis XVI stopped to buy something. The shopkeeper recognized him from his portrait on the coin he tried to pay with and they were recaptured.

It was common in the 18th century to give a newborn baby watered-down wine before it had even tasted milk! Many children would have beer with every meal – not exactly a balanced diet!

Fearsome 18th-century Chinese warriors sometimes dressed in tiger outfits, complete with ears!

The first victim of the guillotine was highwayman Nicolas Pelletier, who was executed in Paris on 25 April 1792.

In 1792, the son of an executioner slipped on the blood running over the cobbles from the guillotine and died of his injuries.

The first people to invest in the steamboat in 1793 insisted on inventor Robert Fulton keeping their names secret in case they were mocked for investing in something that sounded so stupid!

The guillotine was intended to make execution painless.

Copies of important documents were written on the skin of guillotine victims during the French Revolution, including the French constitution of 1793 and The Rights of Man.

Napoleon used flag signals called *semaphore* to send messages from Paris to Rome in under four hours.

During the French Revolution, Marie Tussaud (of Madame Tussaud's wax museums) searched through the baskets of chopped-off heads under the guillotine and made death masks of famous victims.

In 1795, the French government offered a big cash prize for the best idea of how to preserve food for the army. Chef Nicholas Appert suggested airtight metal tins and won the prize! He opened the world's first cannery with his winnings.

King Louis XVI, one of the most famous victims of the guillotine during the French Revolution (1789–1799) actually helped to design it.

Americans call the British 'limeys' because from 1795, British sailors were fed lemons or limes to ward off *scurvy* – a disease caused by a lack of Vitamin C.

During the period called the 'Terror' in the French Revolution, the executioner Sanson guillotined 300 people in just three days.

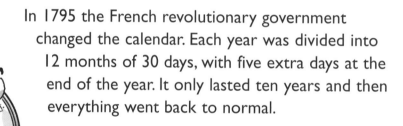

In 1795 the French revolutionary government changed the calendar. Each year was divided into 12 months of 30 days, with five extra days at the end of the year. It only lasted ten years and then everything went back to normal.

The blade of the guillotine fell at 6.5 metres (21 feet) per second. The actual beheading took one 200th of a second.

Dr Joseph Fry of Bristol, England, discovered a method of mass-producing chocolate in 1795. It took another 52 years to come up with the first chocolate bar.

Railings were eventually added to the scaffold on which the guillotine stood, as the vast pools of blood made the floor dangerously slippery for the executioner, who might have fallen off and hurt himself…

The first magician to perform the trick of sawing a woman in half was Count de Grisley in 1799.

Women who used to sit and knit at the foot of the guillotine in the French revolution were called *les tricoteuses* – 'the knitters', sensibly enough.

Martha Washington (wife of George Washington, the first President of the United States) is the only woman whose portrait has ever appeared on a US bank note.

In 1803 the United States purchased Louisiana from France for just 4 cents (2 pence) per acre.

The last criminal to be hanged, drawn and quartered in England was Edward Despard in 1803.

After he was killed at the Battle of Trafalgar in 1805, Admiral Nelson's body was brought back to England in a barrel of French brandy. Sailors on board drank the barrel dry in his memory.

The first tin cans began appearing in shops in 1810. The tin opener wasn't invented until 1860…

The pianist Franz Liszt (1811–1886) received so many requests for locks of his hair that he bought a dog and snipped off patches of its fur to send to his admirers instead!

The White House in Washington DC (home of the President of the United States of America) was originally grey! After the war of 1812 it was burned by Canadian troops; the outside walls were painted white to hide the smoke stains.

King Charles I of England (who was beheaded in 1649) was dug up for an autopsy in 1813. The royal surgeon, Sir Henry Halford, stole a bone from the king's spine and for many years, Halford used it to hold salt on his dining table. How rude!

A carrier pigeon brought news of the Battle of Waterloo's outcome from Belgium to England in 1815.

A blood-draining alternative to leeches, used by 19th-century doctors, was an instrument called a *scarificator* (a bit like a small rolling pin in a holder, with six blades). Rolling it over the skin made six cuts in nice, neat rows.

At the battle of Waterloo in 1815, looters stole teeth from dead bodies and sold them to rich people to use as false teeth. *Waterloo teeth* were a huge hit among European high society.

Saws used by 19th-century surgeons to amputate arms and legs had large notches cut into the blades so that they didn't completely clog up with flesh and gristle.

When Mary Sawyer from Massachusetts, USA took her pet lamb to school one day in 1816, a visitor recorded the commotion in a nursery rhyme: *Mary Had A Little Lamb*.

The poor, particularly children, were often stitched into their clothes for the whole winter as it was never warm enough to take them off, even in bed. The clothes would only be removed in the spring – they must have needed a wash by then!

On 7 February 1821, John Davis, an American seal hunter, became the first man ever to set foot on the continent of Antarctica. Nobody found out until 1955 when his ship's logbook was discovered.

In the early 1800s, Charles Barbier, a captain in the French army, invented 'night writing' to use on the battlefield. The code of raised dots was too hard for the soldiers to use, but led Louis Braille to invent his reading system for the blind in 1821.

The *Claxton earcap* was an arrangement of straps worn over the head in the 19th century to make sticky-out ears grow close to the head. There's no evidence that it worked…what a lot of fuss for nothing!

Napoleon's wallpaper might have killed him… it contained *copper arsenite* and when it became damp, it gave off poisonous vapors. He died in 1821.

Symphony No. 9, written by Ludwig van Beethoven in 1824, is one of the best-known works of Western classical music. Beethovenwas completely deaf when he wrote it.

English physician James Parkinson died in 1824. He was also a revolutionary and fought for the under-priveleged. In his youth he was suspected of being involved in 'The Popgun Plot' – a plot to murder King George III using a poisoned dart! Parkinson's disease was later named after him, but not until 60 years after his death.

Beethoven insisted on conducting the orchestra playing the premiére of his Ninth Symphony in Vienna – despite being deaf. By the end, Beethoven was several beats behind the orchestra.

In 1826, English chemist John Walker was in his laboratory using a stick to mix some chemicals. When he tried to remove a blob of dried mixture from the stick by scraping it against the stone floor, the end of the stick burst into flames…Walker had accidentally invented the match!

In 1826, German composer Felix Mendelssohn left the score for his overture to *A Midsummer Night's Dream* in a cab. Luckily he was able to rewrite every note from memory!

Spanish artist Francisco de Goya, who died in 1828, may have been killed by his own paint. Goya used poisonous mercury and lead in his paints, which slowly built up in his body.

Shaka, leader of the South African Zulu tribe from 1818 to 1828, didn't trust his witch-finders, so he set them a test. He smeared blood on his own house and told them to find the witch who did it. When they found 300 'guilty' people Shaka had the witch-finders put to death.

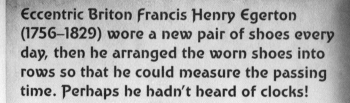

Eccentric Briton Francis Henry Egerton (1756–1829) wore a new pair of shoes every day, then he arranged the worn shoes into rows so that he could measure the passing time. Perhaps he hadn't heard of clocks!

The first person to survive a jump off the Niagara Falls was 23-year-old American Sam Patch, in 1829.

Louis-Antoine, Duke of Angouleme, was King Louis XIX of France for just 20 minutes on 2 August 1830, making his the shortest reign in history.

When the first railways were built in the 1830s, German scientists predicted that passengers would get nosebleeds at speeds over 24 kilometres (15 miles) per hour!

In the 1830s, a British ship arrived at a port in China and fired a cannon as a greeting. Tragically a bystander was killed by one of the cannon shots and the ship's captain was forced to hand over the gunner, who was promptly strangled.

The first fatal railway accident occurred on 17 June 1831 when the boiler exploded on America's first passenger locomotive *The Best Friend of Charleston*.

In the 1830s, beautiful Indian monument the Taj Mahal was about to be torn down. Its marble was to be shipped to London for sale, when word reached them not to do it – the marble market crashed just in time!

One 19th-century American highwayman asked for a copy of his memoirs to be bound in his own skin after his execution.

In 1837, a British judge ruled that if a man kissed a woman against her will, she was legally entitled to bite his nose off.

The Pastry War of 1838 began when Mexican army officers looted a restaurant run by a French pastry chef in Mexico City. The Mexican government refused to pay for the damage, so France declared war.

In 1839, Scottish blacksmith Kirkpatrick Macmillan invented the first pedal bicycle, but his bike had no brakes. In 1842 he was fined for injuring a girl because he couldn't stop.

Britain was the first country to issue postage stamps, in 1840.

The shortest-serving US president was William Henry Harrison, who died in office in 1841, after just 32 days in power.

The mercury used in the hat-making process gave off fumes, which caused symptoms of madness in 19th-century hat makers. This gave us the phrase 'mad as a hatter'.

In May 1842, Scottish craftsman Alexander Bain invented the fax machine. It took another 140 years to become popular.

Antonio de Santa Anna, president of Mexico from 1842 to 1844, held a funeral for his own leg! The limb was amputated after he was wounded during a battle with the French. It was paraded through Mexico City, and buried at a national shrine.

In 1844, Jonathan Walker (who had helped American slaves escape to the Bahamas) became the last person in the United States to be branded in punishment for his crime. The letters 'SS', standing for 'slave stealer', were burned into the palm of his right hand.

A law passed in Britain in 1845 made attempted suicide a crime punishable by death!

Claudius Ash helped give Americans added bite in 1845 when he invented false teeth made of porcelain, mounted with steel springs.

Christmas trees became fashionable in Britain in 1846 when the Illustrated London News showed Queen Victoria and Prince Albert with their young family gathered around one.

19th-century bathers not only covered up with modest bathing outfits, but they were pulled out into the sea in horse drawn carts to avoid attracting attention!

In the first half of the 19th century, ladies carried bottles of *smelling salts* (a mixture of ammonia and perfume) because their tight-fitting corsets caused fainting fits and dizzy spells.

Edgar Allen Poe, the famous American poet and mystery writer (1809–1849), didn't make a good soldier. He committed 66 offences at his military academy, including turning up for parade stark naked!

The Hideous
Age of Empires

1850-1917

Around 1850, Baron Heurteloup invented an artificial leech, rather like a hypodermic syringe, for drawing out blood without the need to maintain an army of live leeches!

Despite his terrifying appearance, James Lucas became a national curiosity – people travelled long distances to see the 'dirtiest man in England'. He never washed and gradually his body went black with grease and grime.

Bottled beer first appeared in 1850.

Over six million visitors – more than a third of Britain's population – attended the Great Exhibition in London's Hyde Park, which ran from May to October 1851. The exhibition was staged in a massive glass house, (The Crystal Palace) and contained 14,000 exhibits.

Small children were sent to clean chimneys because they could easily fit up a narrow flue. To stop them scraping their knees and elbows badly, they had to rub strong salt water into their skin while sitting very near a hot fire. Their employer would stand over them with a cane to make sure they did it properly.

The Crystal Palace, built for the 1851 Great Exhibition in Britain, had 293,655 panes of glass.

In 1852, the height of Mount Everest was calculated at exactly 29,000 feet (8,839 metres). The figure looked like an estimate, so an extra two feet were added on!

The 10th English Duke of Hamilton was so interested in Egyptian mummies, he got a doctor to mummify him and put him into a stone tomb when he died in 1852 – just like an ancient Egyptian pharaoh!

A cholera epidemic in London (1853–4) killed nearly 11,000 people. It resulted in the discovery that cholera comes from dirty water – after that London was given proper sewers.

James Lucas was so scared of being attacked that he lived alone and slept in his kitchen with a gun by his side.

In 1853 Levi Strauss began making trousers for Californian gold miners, using a tough blue material called denim. The copper rivets were added in 1873, and jeans, as we know them today, had arrived!

In 1853, US President Franklin Pierce was arrested for running over an old woman with his horse.

In the 19th century, women wore corsets made of metal to give them the hourglass shape they wanted. Often they were so tight-fitted, they made them faint and damaged their internal organs!

One evening in 1853, American millionaire Cornelius Vanderbilt complained that his French fries were too thick. To teach him a lesson, the chef sliced a potato so thinly and fried it so heavily that it couldn't be cut with a fork. Instead of being annoyed, Vanderbilt loved the new invention of crisps!

The original inspiration for fairground roller coasters was a coal delivery railroad in Summit Hill, Pennsylvania. People would pay to whizz down the 14-kilometre (8.7-mile) downhill track in the 1850s.

In 1854, English Duke Cavendish-Scott-Bentinck created a vast underground network of rooms and tunnels beneath his estate. It included a ballroom and a hydraulic lift but he was so reclusive – he never had any visitors to stay!

A Chinese torture chair from the 19th century has blades sticking up from the armrests and seat, and sticking out from the back. It would be impossible to sit on it without being stabbed – your own weight would push the blades into your flesh.

During the battle of Balaclava in 1854, British soldiers burned the chocolate supplies they were sent as a food boost - it was the only way to stay warm in the freezing Russian weather.

In 1854, Florence Nightingale arrived in Scutari, Istanbul, to work as a nurse during the Crimean War. She soon discovered that amputated limbs were left outside for pigs to eat.

Amongst other meals they tried, English naturalists William and Frank Buckland (father and son) ate stewed flies, mice on toast and a mole! Tasty…

A woman cut the safety cables of an elevator as it climbed a 91-metre (300-foot) tower at New York's *Crystal Palace Exposition* in 1857. The brakes worked, and his new invention was suddenly worth a great deal of money!

When Indian soldiers mutinied in 1857 at the start of the first Indian war of Independence, the British responded savagely. A favourite punishment was to strap a rebel across the mouth of a cannon and fire it.

In the summer of 1858 the smell of untreated sewage almost overwhelmed the people of London. It was so bad that Parliament had to close down!

Thomas Austin released 24 wild rabbits on his property in Victoria, Australia, in October 1859. Within ten years, the rabbit population had exploded, devastating the continent's ecology. Little pests!

Leeches were still used for draining blood during the 19th century. Special 'leech tubes' were used to direct small leeches into awkward areas, such as inside the ears.

Joshua Norton, a failed businessman, proclaimed himself Emperor of the United States in 1859. For 21 years, he went about San Francisco wearing a splendid uniform and carrying a large ceremonial sword.

In 1859 a ship, *The Saint Paul,* left Hong Kong on its voyage to Australia. It was shipwrecked on the way, and all but one of the 326 passengers on board were roasted and eaten by cannibals on the island of Rossel, Papua New Guinea.

Walter Hunt (1796–1859) invented the fountain pen, the sewing machine, the knife sharpener and the ice plough.

In 1859, Jean François Gravelet became the first person to cross the Niagara Falls on a tightrope.

The London Underground (started in 1860) was the world's first underground railway. Instead of drilling tunnels, builders dug trenches at street level and then roofed them over, causing massive disruption across the city.

In the 1860s, the fashion for *crinolines* (stiff, hooped petticoats worn under the skirt) reached its height with many measuring 1.8 metres (6 feet) wide.

Around 315 soldiers serving in the Union Army in the American Civil War (1861–65) died of sunstroke.

During the American Civil War (1861–65), between 33 and 50 per cent of currency in circulation was counterfeit.

American Civil War general Stonewall Jackson had no sense of direction. He became known for leading his troops in complete circles!

Susanna M Salter (America's first woman mayor 1860-61) won her election by a two-thirds majority. She only found out she was running when she reached the voting booth – her name had been submitted without her knowing!

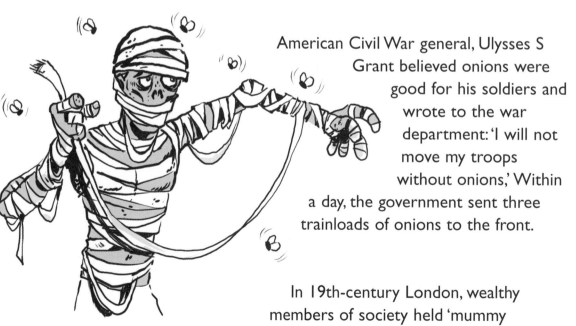

American Civil War general, Ulysses S Grant believed onions were good for his soldiers and wrote to the war department: 'I will not move my troops without onions,' Within a day, the government sent three trainloads of onions to the front.

In 19th-century London, wealthy members of society held 'mummy unwrapping parties'! They were extremely popular – invitations were the hottest tickets in town!

On 4 July 1862, on a rowing trip in the Oxfordshire countryside, mathematician Charles Dodgson told his friend's daughter, Alice Liddell, a fairy tale he had made up for her. Soon after, Dodgson published it as *Alice's Adventures in Wonderland* under the pseudonym Lewis Carroll.

Many of the soldiers in the Confederate Army during the American Civil War didn't know left from right. To teach them to march, officers placed a piece of straw in one boot and a piece of hay in the other, and then shouted: 'Hay foot! Straw foot!'

American inventor William Bullock helped to revolutionize the printing industry with his web rotary printing press, developed in 1863. In a bizarre accident, Bullock was killed by his own invention when he became caught up in one of his machines.

US president Abraham's Lincoln's *Gettysbury Address* speech in 1863 is one of the most quoted speeches in American history, despite being just two minutes long.

'They couldn't hit an elephant at this dist…' were the last words of General John Sedgwick, killed in battle during the American Civil War in 1864.

Alfred Nobel invented dynamite in 1867. He later deeply regretted inventing the explosive because of its use in warfare and used the fortune he earned from it to set up the Nobel Peace Prize.

Blood was a popular cure for epilepsy in England in the 1700s and in Switzerland until the 1860s.

Public hangings were stopped in England in 1868. They were so crowded that too many people were hurt or killed in the crush to see the action!

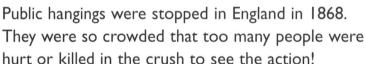

The world's first ever traffic light was installed on 10 December 1868 outside the Houses of Parliament in London, England. Unfortunately it exploded on 2 January 1869, injuring the policeman operating it.

During the siege of Paris in 1870–1, the city ran out of food. Restaurants served cat, dog and rat!

Ancient Egyptian mummies were used as fuel in the 19th century. There were so many around, that they were burned to power trains. Poor people in Egypt burned mummy bandages to heat their houses.

A book was published in 1870 which suggested that spinach contains ten times as much iron as it really does.

The two half-sisters of playwright Oscar Wilde burned to death at a party in 1871. They walked too close to a fire and their huge *crinolines* (petticoats) caught light.

Englishwoman Mary Ann Cotton was hanged in 1873 for poisoning at least 15 people with arsenic. She got away with it by moving around the country to areas where she wasn't known, before killing again.

In the early 1870s, the western frontier town of Palisade, Nevada, USA, was famed as the roughest, toughest town in the Wild West! Whenever a train pulled into the station, passengers were shocked to see gunfights, stabbings, bank robberies and attacks…but in fact they were all staged to maintain the town's reputation!

In 1872, Joshua Coppersmith was arrested for trying to fool people into buying shares in a company that would make equipment that sent voice messages over a wire. Within four years, Alexander Graham Bell invented the telephone. How unfair!

In 1873, Eli Randolph of New York patented a 'moustache guard'. It was made of rubber and held in place by two curved prongs that were inserted into the nostrils. Randolph claimed it protected the moustache from food and drink and made kissing more hygienic.

Thomas Edison accidentally discovered photocopying when he was using paraffin to try to improve telegraph tape in 1875.

On the Danish islands of Amak and Moen, public beheadings were well attended in the 19th century! They were particularly popular with people suffering from epilepsy, who would crowd around the scaffold, trying to catch the blood in cups so they could use it to treat the condition.

American dentist George Green revolutionized his profession in 1875 with the invention of the electric dental drill. Green's innovation could reach speeds of up to 3,000 rotations per minute…ouch!

A horse named Comanche was the only survivor from the losing side at the Battle of Little Bighorn on 26 June 1876 in the USA.

Both Alexander Graham Bell and his rival Elisha Gray filed their applications for the telephone at the US Patent Office on the same day, 14 February 1876. Bell got there an hour or so before Gray – luckily for him!

Heinz launched tomato ketchup in 1876. The word comes from the Chinese *ke-tsiap*, a sauce made from pickled fish.

In 1877, Thomas Edison invented the music-playing *phonograph*. In the same year, Chester Greenwood patented earmuffs! It was a big year for inventions!

In the 19th century, prisoners were holed up in filthy, crowded ships on the river Thames. In the daytime they were let out to do horrible tasks, like cleaning away sewage.

Naturalist William Buckland liked exotic food. Among his favourite meals were elephant's trunk soup, roast giraffe and panther chops. He even tried earwigs once, but complained they tasted rather bitter.

Australian outlaw Ned Kelly dressed in homemade armour during a shootout with police on 26 June 1880. He forgot to cover his legs though, and was shot 28 times.

The citizens of San Francisco treated 'Emperor' Joshua Norton with great respect. When he died in 1880, nearly 30,000 people filed past his coffin to pay their respects. He wasn't really an emperor, just very eccentric!

Travellers to Mongolia in the 19th century were horrified to discover prisoners kept in coffins for years and years as punishment.

When trying to remove an assassin's bullet from the chest of the American President James Garfield in 1881, doctors poking their fingers into the wound accidentally punctured the president's liver.

Ice cream shop owner Ed Berners of Wisconsin, USA, invented the ice cream sundae in 1881. He only served his treat on Sundays.

Flogging (whipping) was still allowed as punishment in the British army until 1881. Other European armies had given up on it long before.

Electric lights were first used on Christmas trees in 1882 in New York.

At Dr John Harvey Kellogg's health clinic, which he ran during the 1880s, he insisted that underweight people stay in bed all day and eat up to 26 meals a day. They were not allowed to take any physical exercise – their teeth were even brushed by nurses!

The inventor Alexander Graham Bell offered President Garfield's doctors a metal detector so they could find the bullet in his body. The machine didn't work because the bed he was in had a metal frame.

If a man in the British army in the 19th century struck an officer or a doctor he could be killed. Sometimes the victim would have to stand or kneel next to the coffin he would be put into, and would then be shot.

Ebenezer Place in Scotland, built in 1883, is the shortest street in the world. The street is 2 metres (6.5 feet) long and has just one address: 1 Ebenezer Place.

'Go on, get out – last words are for fools who haven't said enough' revolutionary philosopher Karl Marx said to his housekeeper from his deathbed, in 1883. She had asked him if he wanted to say something that she could record for posterity. He died soon afterwards.

The game of table tennis began as an after-dinner amusement for wealthy Victorian men in the 1880s. A line of books formed the net, a champagne cork was the ball, and a cigar box lid was the bat!

A murderer called John Lee was sentenced to hang in 1884. But each of the three times the executioner tried, the trapdoor failed to open. Eventually, he was sent to prison instead.

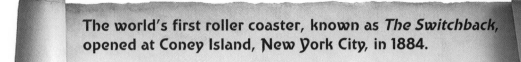

The world's first roller coaster, known as *The Switchback*, opened at Coney Island, New York City, in 1884.

Coca-Cola was invented in 1885, by American pharmacist, John Stith Pemberton. The original ingredients included wine and cocaine and it was sold as a medicine.

Baunscheidtism was a common treatment for various illnesses in the second half of the 19th century. It was developed in Germany and involved rubbing poisonous oils onto the skin, which would then be punctured using a round instrument fitted with many sharp spikes.

The original Jumbo, a circus elephant, was killed on 15 September 1885 after being hit by a locomotive in Ontario, Canada.

The Eiffel Tower was built from 18,038 pieces of iron, using two and a half million rivets between 1887 and 1889. Despite the open frame, only one man died in its construction.

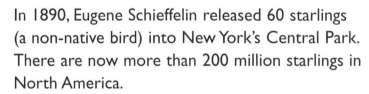

In 1888, an Egyptian farmer discovered an ancient cat cemetery containing 10,000 cat mummies. The entire haul was shipped to Liverpool in England, where the mummies were ground up and sold as fertilizer.

Jack the Ripper mutilated and killed a number of women in the Whitechapel area of London in 1888. The identity of the murderer is still unproven. to this day.

In the late 19th century, the fashion for women wearing exotic bird feathers in their hats brought some species to the brink of extinction.

In 1890, Eugene Schieffelin released 60 starlings (a non-native bird) into New York's Central Park. There are now more than 200 million starlings in North America.

A Victorian doctor invented a trap for *tapeworms* (parasitic worms that live in the human gut). It was a little metal cage, baited with something tasty for the tapeworms. The patient had to swallow it on a string and wait for the tapeworm to spring the trap, when it would be pulled out of the body. Some people choked to death in the process!

In the 1890s, Emperor Menelek of Ethiopia was informed of a new method of execution in the USA – the electric chair. Impressed, he immediately ordered three to be sent to his palace. There was no electricity in Ethiopia at the time, but rather than waste the chairs, he used one as a throne!

In 1892 Italy raised the minimum age for marriage for girls to 12 years old.

In 1892, Parisian stamp collector Hector Giroux, murdered businessman Gaston Leroux, for the sake of a Hawaiian stamp from 1851 worth only 1 pence (2 cents).

In Rhode Island, USA in 1892, Mercy Brown's father had her body dug up after her death, burnt her heart and mixed it into a drink for her brother. He believed she was a vampire and was killing his son, who was actually dying of tuberculosis.

When Henry Ziegland of Texas, USA, walked out on his girlfriend in 1893, she was so angry she got her brother to shoot him. The bullet missed and embedded itself in the trunk of a tree. Twenty years later, Ziegland decided to remove the tree from his property using dynamite. In the explosion, the bullet flew out and killed him.

The first country to give women the vote was New Zealand, in 1893.

French novelist Guy de Maupassant (1850–1893) hated the Eiffel Tower, but ate lunch at its restaurant every day. When asked why, he answered that it was the one place in Paris from which you couldn't see the tower!

In 1894, distinguished scientist Lord Kelvin declared that radio had no future. He also predicted that heavier-than-air flying machines were impossible.

The world's first comic strip character 'The Yellow Kid' (first printed in 1894) was not a conventional superhero. He was a bald, jug-eared child with a goofy grin and a yellow complexion – but he was the first to use speech balloons.

When X-rays were invented in 1895, many people were worried that it would soon be possible to create X-ray spectacles. One company even started manufacturing 'X-ray-proof' underwear!

In Victorian Britain, people who couldn't afford a proper burial were buried in paupers' graveyards. These were so crowded that often the bodies poked up through the ground and gave off a horrible smell.

The first-ever automobile race was staged in France in 1895. Competitors drove from Paris to Bordeaux.

The shortest war in recorded history was fought between Britain and Zanzibar in 1896. Zanzibar surrendered after 38 minutes.

Archduke Karl Ludwig of Austria was deeply religious. On a pilgrimage to the Holy Land in 1896, he insisted on drinking from the River Jordan, but it poisoned him and he died within a few weeks.

In the 19th century, mummy bandages were often used to make paper. This became illegal after an outbreak of the deadly disease cholera in America was traced to mummy-paper that had been used to wrap food!

In 1897, Belgian Count Karnice-Karnicki invented a mechanism that could detect chest movements occurring in a 'corpse' in a coffin. It set off warning bells and raised a flag over the grave to alert people to the premature burial.

In 1898, fourteen years before the doomed liner *Titanic* sailed and sank, Morgan Robertson wrote a novel about a huge 'unsinkable' ship called *Titan*. On a cold April night the fictional liner hits an iceberg and sinks…spooky!

During the 1898–1899 siege of Baler in the Philippines, 50 Spaniards held out for a whole year against 2,000 Filipinos, not realizing that the Spanish-Filipino War was actually over!

In 1899, France passed a law banning people from dumping their dead animals in the River Seine. A dog cemetery built on the edge of the river now has more than 40,000 pets buried in it including: cats, mice, birds, fish, a racehorse, a lion and a monkey!

In 1900, a 39,000-year-old, perfectly preserved, wooly mammoth was discovered on the banks of the Beresovka River in Siberia. Scientists found buttercups in its mouth!

'Mountain man' John Johnson (1824–1900) married an Indian squaw of the *Flathead* tribe. When she was killed and scalped by another tribe, Johnson began hunting down its members, looking for revenge. He scalped them and ate their livers raw, earning him the nickname 'Liver-eating Johnson'.

Eugene Hollander performed the world's first facelift in Berlin in 1901, on a Polish aristocrat.

Gustave Whitehead from Connecticut, USA, built an aircraft in which he claims to have flown half a mile in August 1901. If true, his would be the first ever flight!

The first recorded use of a getaway car was on 26 October 1901 in Paris, when three robbers drove off after stealing from a shop.

When train robber Thomas 'Black Jack' Ketchum was hanged in 1901 in New Mexico, the executioners miscalculated the drop and the rope decapitated him. His head was sewn back onto his body, so he could be buried properly.

On a 1902 hunting trip, American President Teddy Roosevelt took pity on an old bear and refused to shoot her. New York shop owner Morris Michtom commemorated the event by making the world's first 'teddy bear' – named after the president.

The men of the *Bontoc Igorot* tribe in the Philippines added an extra tattoo to their hands for every person they killed. This continued until the early 20th century.

When the 1000-year-old bell tower in St Mark's Square in Venice, Italy, collapsed in 1902 the only casualty was the caretaker's cat that had gone back inside for its breakfast.

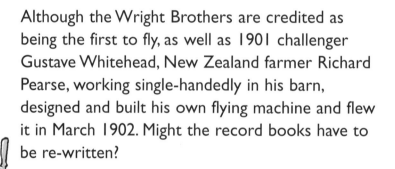

Although the Wright Brothers are credited as being the first to fly, as well as 1901 challenger Gustave Whitehead, New Zealand farmer Richard Pearse, working single-handedly in his barn, designed and built his own flying machine and flew it in March 1902. Might the record books have to be re-written?

Tsar Nicholas II of Russia's son, Alexei, was born in 1904. He was born with the disease *haemophilia*, which prevents blood clotting normally, so if he got a cut it would bleed and bleed for hours.

The board game *Monopoly* was invented in 1904 by Elizabeth Magie from Maryland, USA, who called it *The Landlord's Game*.

Teabags were invented by accident in 1904 when New York tea merchant Thomas Sullivan began sending out samples to his clients in silk bags with a drawstring, rather than in more expensive tins. Customers placed the bags in their cups, thinking the tea was supposed to be brewed that way.

Tsar Nicholas II sought the help of the mystic healer, Rasputin in 1905 to try to cure his son of *haemophilia*.

In 1904 over 100 protesting Russian workers were killed and more than 300 injured by palace guards on 'Bloody Sunday', which triggered the 1905 Russian Revolution.

The ice lolly was accidentally invented by 11-year-old Frank Epperson in San Francisco, USA. In 1905, he left his glass of lemonade, containing a stirrer, outside. In the morning, it had frozen solid.

1906 was an important year for breakfast! William Kellogg launched his *Cornflakes* and George Washington invented instant coffee.

In 1908 a meteorite struck the earth with enough force to destroy an entire city. The same thing happened again in 1947. Luckily, both fell in remote, uninhabited areas of Siberia.

The Eiffel Tower was supposed to be taken down in 1909 but it was kept because it was a useful high place for radio antennae.

In 1909, Louis Blériot became the first man to fly from England to France. His wooden aeroplane was tied together with piano strings! The engine only managed to hold out because a rain shower cooled it off.

Kellogg's *Cornflakes* were an accidental discovery. William Kellogg forgot about a pot of boiled wheat he'd left heating on the stove. When he flattened the dried-out wheat with a roller, each grain came out as a large, thin flake.

It's an urban myth that Thomas Crapper (1836–1910) invented the flushing toilet! He was simply a successful London plumber with his own brand of toilets.

On 15 April 1912, the *Titanic* sank on its maiden voyage when it struck an iceberg. There were 2,227 people on board, but only 705 survived.

The best thing since sliced bread could be…the bread-slicing machine! Frederick Rohwedder invented it in 1912.

The world's first crossword puzzle was published in the *New York World* newspaper in 1913. It was invented by Englishman, Arthur Wynne.

On 18 August 1913 at a casino in Monte Carlo, the roulette ball landed in a black slot 26 times in a row. The odds for this happening are one in 136,823,184.

The zip was invented in 1913, but many people thought it would lead to bad behaviour because it was so easy to remove clothes with a zip! They weren't widely used until the 1950s.

Stubby the pit bull terrier served with the 102nd Infantry in the trenches of France during the First World War. He helped locate wounded soldiers and gave early warning of enemy artillery fire. He eventually earned the rank of Sergeant!

No one can know exactly how many people were killed in World War I (1914–1918). Historians believe that about 10 million soldiers were killed and 20 million wounded. The scale of its destruction was greater than any previous conflict.

The French soldiers arrived at the battlefield of the Marne in September 1914 by taxi.

Cher Ami was a legendary homing pigeon of World War I, who received the Cross of War award for delivering 12 vital messages during the conflict. In his final mission, the brave bird delivered a message despite having been shot!

Einstein's theory of relativity (developed between 1907 and 1915) was partly inspired by a man who fell off a roof in Berlin.

Trench foot was a common affliction for soldiers in World War I – their feet were always wet and soon rotted.

Margaret Sanger was jailed for one month in 1916 for setting up the first birth control clinic in the USA.

In 1916, fifty-five per cent of the world's cars were Model T Fords.

The British royal family is partly German. They changed their last name from Saxe-Coburg-Gotha in 1917 when Britain was at war with Germany. King George V decided that the family would take the name of his castle, Windsor.

During World War I, the British developed a new weapon which they referred to as a 'water carrier' to keep it secret. It was later shortened to 'tank' and the name stuck.

Tsar Nicholas II was the last tsar of Russia. He was known as 'Bloody Nicholas' because of all the bloodshed during his reign. The Russian Revolution ended his rule in 1917 and in 1918, Nicholas and his entire family were shot.

The most feared pilot of World War I was German, Manfred von Richthofen, also known as The Red Baron, who shot down over 80 enemy planes.

Cats became vital companions to soldiers on the front line during World War I. They helped keep down the rat population in the cramped and dirty trenches.

Dutch exotic dancer Mata Hari was accused of being a spy during World War I and was executed by firing squad in 1917. Her head was embalmed and kept in the Museum of Anatomy in Paris until the year 2000 when curators discovered it had disappeared, along with the rest of her remains!

During World War I soldiers often lived in terrible conditions in the trenches, and suffered with rashes, fever, sores, inflamed eyes, body lice and sickness.

In a town called Fatima, Portugal, in 1917, three children claimed to have seen a holy vision. They were imprisoned and told they'd be boiled in oil unless they admitted they were lying. They claimed that three prophetic secrets had been revealed to them. One of the children – Sister Lucia dos Santos – died in 2005 and is on the list to be made a Saint.

The Hideous Modern World

1918–Present

The influenza pandemic of 1918–1919 was the worst of all time, killing approximately 25 million people. That's more than the number killed in World War I.

The word 'robot' was first used in a play by Czech writer Karel Capek, first staged in 1920. In Czech, *robota* means 'forced labour'.

King Alexandros I of Greece died in 1920 from blood poisoning, after being bitten by his pet monkey.

Vatican City – at just 44 hectares (18 acres) in size – became the smallest independent nation in the world in 1921. It even has its own army!

In 1921, the British Empire controlled about a quarter of the world's total land area, ruling over 458 million people.

In the early 1920s the Italian fascists would intimidate their socialist enemies by feeding them large amounts of castor oil (a laxative) then tying them to a lamp post so that they couldn't move away.

The last of the true *Barbary* lions, famed for their appearances in the Roman Colosseum, was killed in the Atlas Mountains in 1922.

In 1924, the State of Nevada, USA, introduced the gas chamber as a more humane form of execution. Its first victim was convicted murderer Gee Jong.

The first successful helicopter flight was by the Argentinian engineer Raul Pateras Pescara de Castelluccio in January 1924. He flew for ten minutes.

After the death of Lenin in 1924, his brain was entrusted to a respected doctor who (it was hoped) would be able to revive the Soviet leader...

Chicago gangster Dion O'Banion was given a lavish funeral in 1924, with 10,000 mourners paying their respects. The biggest and most expensive wreath came from Al Capone – the gangster who had ordered O'Banion's murder!

The *frisbee* was invented in 1925 by American college students when they began tossing and catching the empty circular pie tins of the Frisbie Baking Company.

During the 1920s, Tokyo's Prefect of Police ordered that all kissing scenes be deleted from imported Hollywood movies before being shown in the city's cinemas.

In 1925 a dog started a war between Greece and Bulgaria! The canine belonged to a Greek soldier and it wandered over the border. The soldier went to retrieve it and was shot by a Bulgarian border guard. In retaliation, Greece invaded Bulgaria.

When Hollywood mogul Harry M. Warner, of Warner Brothers, was told of the possibility of movies with sound, he asked: 'Who wants to hear actors talk?'

Modern success in blood transfusion is largely due to the work of Russian doctor Alexander Bogdanov, who hoped blood transfusion would provide the secret to eternal youth. He claimed that his eyesight improved and his hair loss stopped after transfusing blood into himself from 1925 onwards.

In 1926, a waiter in Budapest left a suicide note in the form of a crossword. Police had to call on help from the public in order to solve it.

Transatlantic phone calls first became possible in 1927.
They were around half the cost of a car for just 3 minutes!

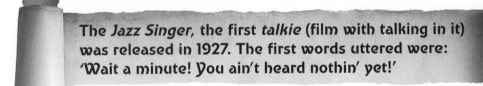

The *Jazz Singer*, the first *talkie* (film with talking in it)
was released in 1927. The first words uttered were:
'Wait a minute! You ain't heard nothin' yet!'

Toilet rolls first appeared in the shops in 1928.

During the Prohibition era in America (1920–1933) which banned
alcohol, a man accused of selling it illegally had to be acquitted
because the jury drank the evidence! The jurors claimed
they had sampled the drink to determine if it
contained alcohol – which it did!

In 1928, Walter Diemer, the inventor of bubble
gum, never received a penny in royalties for
his creation. When asked about it, he said:
'I've made kids happy around the world.
How many people can make that claim?'

The world's first antibiotic was created by accident in
1928. Scottish scientist Alexander Fleming was washing
dishes when he noticed that a flake of mould had fallen
into some bacteria he was growing, and killed them. From
the mould, he extracted *penicillin*.

The yo-yo was invented in the Philippines centuries ago – possibly for use as a weapon! Its history as a children's toy began in 1928 when Pedro Flores opened a factory making them in California.

In 1929, Clarence Birdseye launched the first ever range of frozen foods. He got the idea during expeditions to Labrador, Canada, where he saw natives freezing their food in order to preserve it.

Fritz von Opel, a German car builder, became the first person to fly by rocket power in 1929. He stayed in the air for 75 seconds!

In 1929, the Soviet Union decreed that each week would have just five days. In 1932, it decreed six days. By 1940, the seven-day week had been restored!

Fascist dictator Benito Mussolini was annoyed by the Tower of Pisa leaning over. During the 1930s, he ordered the foundation to be filled with concrete to straighten it. As a result, the tower sank further into the soil!

The first flight into the stratosphere took place in 1931, when Auguste Piccard and Charles Knipfer took off in their balloon from Augsburg, Germany.

When Thomas Edison (inventor of the electric light bulb) died in October 1931, lights were dimmed for one minute throughout the USA as a sign of respect.

On 5 February 1933, Americans celebrated the end of Prohibition by drinking 1.5 million barrels of beer.

In 1935, Dr Egas Moniz of Portugal developed the *lobotomy* (a type of brain surgery). A mallet was used to drive an ice pick through the top of the eye socket to cut the lobes at the front of the brain, as a way to cure mental illness. It Sounds more like torture!

Henry Wellcome, founder of the Wellcome Foundation (a medical research charity since 1936) made a large collection of medical curiosities, including pieces of human skin with interesting tattoos, instruments of torture and scary medical instruments.

The last public execution in the USA took place in Kentucky, in 1936. Over 20,000 people gathered to watch the hanging of convicted murderer Rainey Bethea.

Edward VIII of England was one of Britain's shortest-reigning monarchs and the only one to voluntarily give up the throne. The reason? So he could marry the American divorcée Wallis Simpson. He reigned between January and December 1936.

San Francisco's Golden Gate Bridge opened on 27 May 1937. The US navy had asked that it be painted black with yellow stripes for better visibility, but it was painted orange to blend with the scenery.

Innkeeper Ruth Wakefield invented chocolate chip cookies during the 1930s. Making some cookies one day, she cut up a chocolate bar and mixed the chunks in the batter. She expected them to melt and make chocolate cookies but instead she got butter biscuits studded with chocolate pieces.

Eleven construction workers were killed during the building of the Golden Gate Bridge and another 19 were saved thanks to a safety net.

A radio broadcast of HG Wells' story War of the Worlds caused mass panic in 1938 when listeners mistook it for real news that aliens were invading Earth!

The bloodiest conflict in history was World War II (1939–1945), during which over 54 million people died.

When Swiss engineer George de Mestral went walking in the mountains near Lausanne during the 1940s, he noticed that *burrs* (a type of seed) often got stuck to his woollen trousers which inspired him to invent Velcro.

The first Allied air raid on Germany in World War II killed the only elephant in Berlin Zoo.

In 1940 Peter Goldmark, a Hungarian born American engineer, developed the first ever colour television. It was a mechanical system that rotated the colours red green and blue.

The biggest air battle in history was the Battle of Britain, which lasted from 10 July to 31 October 1940. It involved over 6,000 German and British planes.

During World War II, both the occupying German army and the French Resistance movement used the long passageways of the Paris *catacombs* (underground cemeteries) to move around in secret.

In the 1940s, Californian law made it illegal for people to dress as a member of the opposite sex.

The youngest US serviceman in World War II was just 12 years old. He lied about his age so that he could fight.

The last German emperor, Kaiser Wilhelm II (1859–1941) was born with a withered left arm. Photographs always show his left hand resting on a sword or holding a pair of gloves to hide the deformity.

During the early 1940s, American engineer James Wright was trying to help the war effort by developing a synthetic alternative to rubber when he accidentally invented *Silly Putty*. This turned out to be the greatest triumph of his career!

Around 1941 British fighter pilot John Cunningham bacame famous for having shot down 14 enemy bombers at night. A rumour began circulating that he ate lots of carrots to develop his night vision!

In 1941, American inventor Percy Spencer was working on a radar machine when he noticed that the chocolate bar in his pocket had melted. He tried holding a bag of popcorn in front of the machine and watched it pop! The microwave oven was built in 1947.

During the siege of Leningrad, Russia, in 1941–2, people ate all the rats and pets in the city, and stripped the bark from all trees within 32 kilometres (20 miles) to eat.

The term 'bug' as applied to computers can be traced to 1943, when naval officer Grace Hopper encountered a glitch in her machine. The system, it turned out, had a bug – a real one! A moth had made its way inside her computer. Since then, 'bug' has meant any kind of fault in a computer.

In 1943, the US armed forces became the world's largest ice cream manufacturer, producing 363 million litres (80 million gallons) of ice cream per year for American troops.

The highly dangerous psychedelic effects of the drug LSD were discovered in April 1943. Swiss chemist Albert Hofmann was developing the drug as a possible medicine.

The island of Jersey was the only part of Great Britain to be occupied by Nazi Germany during World War II between 1940 and 1945.

Until the 1940s, the Mundurucú tribe of the Amazon tattooed all children from the age of six to sixteen, adding stripes, bands and patterns slowly over time until the entire body was tattooed to look like a bird.

During World War II, the Russian army used dogs strapped with explosives to blow up German tanks.

In 1944 scientists at The Rockefeller University, New York discovered that DNA is the material that carries the genetic information that we inherit.

On 6 June 1944, known as D-Day, the Allied armies invaded Nazi-occupied France at Normandy. To alert their members of the landing, the French Resistance used the coded message 'John has a long moustache'. Genius!

During the Battle of Monte Cassino in early 1944, the 2nd Polish Corps had a brown bear named *Wojtek* who helped move boxes of ammunition.

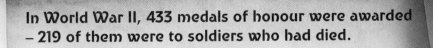

In World War II, 433 medals of honour were awarded – 219 of them were to soldiers who had died.

The world's biggest food fight occurs every year on the last Wednesday of August. Since 1944, the town of Buŀol in Spain has hosted an annual festival called *La Tomatina* in which 40,000 people pelt each other with tomatoes!

Six bomber crewmen were killed for every one who was only injured in World War II.

The military administrators of the atomic bomb project at Los Alamos in the 1940s, New Mexico, were so concerned about security that they only hired illiterate people for maintenance jobs at the plant.

Ice cream was so popular with US forces that, in 1945, the navy built a 'floating ice cream parlor' that could produce 45 litres (10 gallons) of ice cream per second!

During World War II, the US army planned to use Mexican *free-tailed bats* as 'bat bombs' to drop explosives over Japan.

Pioneering cosmetic surgeon Archibald McIndoe treated hundreds of young soldiers who suffered facial burns during World War II. McIndoe's techniques were often entirely experimental. For this reason his former patients called themselves 'The Guinea Pig Club'.

King George V of England died on 26 January 1946 at 11.55pm. His doctor gave him a lethal injection so that he would die before midnight and his death could be announced in the morning *Times* instead of in a less prestigious afternoon newspaper.

French engineer Louis Reard launched the bikini on 5 July 1946 at a Paris fashion show. It was named after *Bikini Atoll* – the site of atomic weapon tests.

The first pilot to travel faster than the speed of sound was Chuck Yeager of the US Air Force. In 1947, he took his experimental X-1 rocket-powered plane to supersonic speed in the skies above Muroc Air Force Base, California.

Gangster Al Capone's business card said he was a used furniture dealer.

A 1947 study found that during World War II only about 15–25 per cent of American soldiers ever fired their weapons in combat.

In 1948, brothers Dick and Mac McDonald opened a restaurant in California that sold only hamburgers, fries and milkshakes produced on a continuous basis rather than made to order. Dick called it 'fast food' and called the restaurant *McDonalds*.

Simon was a ship's cat on HMS *Amethyst* in 1949. He was so good at killing rats and boosting morale among the men that he was awarded the 'Animal VC', the 'Dickin Medal' and the rank of 'Able Seacat'!

Witchcraft laws were not lifted in Britain until 1951.

In 1952, George Jorgensen, a former GI in the US army, was the first person to have gender-reassignment surgery to become a woman called Christine.

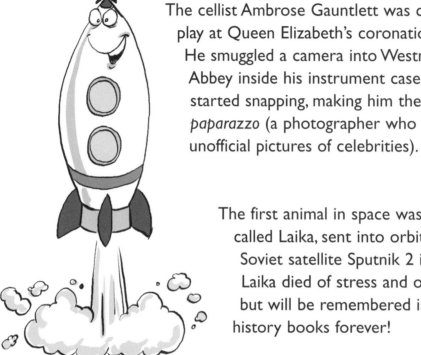

The cellist Ambrose Gauntlett was chosen to play at Queen Elizabeth's coronation in 1953. He smuggled a camera into Westminster Abbey inside his instrument case and started snapping, making him the first *paparazzo* (a photographer who takes unofficial pictures of celebrities).

The first animal in space was a dog called Laika, sent into orbit in the Soviet satellite Sputnik 2 in 1957. Laika died of stress and overheating, but will be remembered in the history books forever!

When Elvis Presley appeared on the *Ed Sullivan Show* in January 1957, the producers were concerned that his hip-swaying might damage its image as a family show, so they decided to show him from the waist up only. This censorship gave him his new nickname: 'Elvis the Pelvis'!

During the Russian occupation of East Berlin in the 1950s and 1960s up to a third of the population were spying on the rest of the citizens.

Sir Edmund Hillary and his team arrived at the South Pole in 1958. His expedition made him the first overland explorer to do so since 1912. New Zealander Hillary was also the first person to reach the peak of Mount Everest.

The Barbie doll, created in 1959, was named after Barbara, the daughter of the doll's creator Ruth Handler.

In 1959, Chester Carlson offered IBM his photocopier machine. After carrying out some research, IBM declined the offer, as they believed very few people would use it. Today, around three billion photocopies are made every day worldwide!

In the 1960s, at the height of the Cold War, both the US and Soviet navies conscripted teams of dolphins. Their duties included locating underwater mines, finding lost equipment and blowing up enemy ships and submarines.

Wilson Greatbatch invented the first ever *pacemaker* (a device which stimulates and regulates a person's heartbeat) by accident in 1960 while he was working on a device to record a patient's heartbeat.

In 1961, Martin Graetz and Alan Kotok, two students at Massachusetts Institute of Technology, created the world's first computer game, *Spacewar*.

The Brazilian *Wari tribe* was still practising *cannibalism* (humans eating humans) until the 1960s. They believed they really had to force down slices of human flesh, even if it made them sick!

Inspired by ancient skulls with holes drilled in them, a Dutch doctor used an electric drill to make a hole in his own head in 1962. He believed it would keep him young. Maybe, but he was locked away in a mental hospital as a result.

Remarkable coincidences surround the assassinations of US Presidents Abraham Lincoln (1865) and John F Kennedy (1963). Both men were assassinated on a Friday, in the presence of their wives, by a bullet to the back of the head, with the assailant fleeing to a warehouse.

On 9 November 1965, the biggest power failure in history caused a nine-hour blackout across north-eastern USA and southern Canada. There was a surge in the birth rate nine months later...

In 1969, the US Navy commissioned a study into the 'aerodynamics of the self-suspended flare'. The research project, which cost $375,000 (£190,013) concluded that the Frisbee was not feasible as military hardware!

During a pre-flight check, a cockroach was found on the Apollo 12 spacecraft launched in 1969, but there was no trace of it when the craft returned to Earth.

The Football War was a six-day war sparked by a fight between fans from El Salvador and Honduras in Central America, after a match in July 1969. Two thousand people died in the conflict.

In 1970, an Arizona lawyer filed a lawsuit for $100,000 (£50,653) damages against God on behalf of his secretary, Betty Penrose. Ms Penrose accused God of negligence in allowing a lightning bolt to strike her home. She won when God failed to appear in court!

A grave robber who tried to rob a pharaoh's tomb in a pyramid caused the roof to fall in! He was trapped with his hand in the coffin, when the coffin lid was slammed down by the falling roof. He skeleton was discovered by archaeologists excavating the tomb in 1970.

The first email message was sent in 1971 by Ray Tomlinson, an employee at a technology research company.

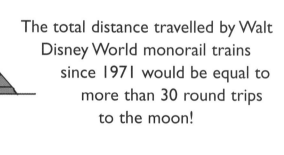

The total distance travelled by Walt Disney World monorail trains since 1971 would be equal to more than 30 round trips to the moon!

For Japanese soldier Shoichi Yokoi, World War II ended on 24 January 1972 when he came out of hiding on Guam Island, where he had been living in a cave for 28 years.

In 1972 a diamond was discovered in Africa that has 969 carats! It's called 'The Star of Sierra Leone'.

In 1972 a plane crashed in the Andes with 45 people on board. Some of the survivors lived by eating the other passengers who had been killed. Those who refused to do so died of starvation before rescuers arrived 70 days later.

The ultimate mafia film 'The Godfather' was first released in 1972. It has since been rated as the second greatest film in American cinematic history after 'Citizen Kane'.

In 1974, US inventor Art Fry invented the Post-it note to prevent slips of paper used to mark his place in his hymn book falling out.

In 1974, *The Guinness Book of World Records* had its own entry from when it set a record as the fastest selling book in the world.

On 18 March 1974, Britain's *Daily Mirror* became the first mass-circulation newspaper to picture a naked streaker on its front page.

The Khmer Rouge regime which ruled Cambodia from 1975 to 1979 killed between 1.7 and 2.3 million people. Many victims were forced to dig their own graves before being killed with axe handles, hammers, spades or sharpened bamboo sticks to save bullets.

The worst aeroplane crash in history occurred on the ground! Two Boeing 747 jumbo jets collided in Tenerife on 27 March 1977. Nearly 600 people were killed.

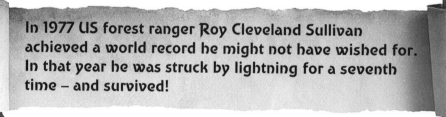

In 1977 US forest ranger Roy Cleveland Sullivan achieved a world record he might not have wished for. In that year he was struck by lightning for a seventh time – and survived!

The final victim of the guillotine was murderer Hamida Djandoubi, who was beheaded in Marseilles, France on 10 September 1977.

The first successful pedal-powered aircraft was the *Gossamer Condor*, created by Paul MacCready in 1977. The aircraft was made of very light materials and flew a distance of 5 kilometres (3 miles).

In 1978, after a ten year effort, the highly infectious disease, *smallpox*, was finally eradicated. It was the first disease to be wiped out by human efforts.

In 1979, former teacher Janice Brown completed the first long distance solar-powered flight when she flew *Solar Challenger* for 10 kilometers (6 miles) in Arizona, USA.

The board game *Trivial Pursuit* was invented by three Canadians in 1979 in just 45 minutes. It took a further three years to sell the idea.

The longest ever jail sentence was 10,000 years. The sentence was passed on Dudley Wayne Kyzer in 1981 for a triple murder.

The first person to receive an artificial heart was Barney Clark in 1982. It was made of aluminium and plastic and kept him alive for 112 more days.

In 1982, researchers at a Japanese laboratory used superglue to fix a crack in the fish tank. They were surprised to see fingerprints suddenly appearing on the glass of the tank. Today, police regularly use superglue fumes to reveal fingerprints.

Many physicists deny that *ball lightning* (a floating ball of lightning) exists at all. But in 1982, one was spotted whizzing through one of the world's top physics laboratories – The Cavendish Laboratory in Cambridge, England.

In 1985, NASA estimated the probability of an accident happening to the space shuttle as 1 in 100,000. Against the odds, on 28 January 1986 – the 25th shuttle mission – *The Challenger* exploded after take-off, killing all seven astronauts.

In 1988, a lock of Admiral Horatio Nelson's hair was sold for £5,575 ($11,014) at a UK auction.

After the execution of Romanian leader Nicolae Ceausescu in 1989, his tomb was guarded day and night because many people thought he was a vampire.

During the civil war in Liberia, Africa of 1989–1996, General Joshua Milton Blahyi was famous for leading his army into battle naked – except for his boots and gun. His nickname was 'General Butt-Naked'!

The world's first ice hotel was constructed in 1990 in Sweden. It has more than 80 rooms, a bar, reception area and church. The hotel melts every April and has to be rebuilt for guests the following winter.

In 1993, police in Oregon, USA, recruited a pot-bellied pig called Harley whom they trained to sniff out illegal drugs.

Bill Clinton, President of the United States from 1993–2001, only ever sent two emails. One was to John Glenn when he was aboard the space shuttle and the other was a test of the email system.

Ebay.com founder, Pierre Omidyar, originally wanted to call his company *EchoBay.com* but the name was already being used by the gold mining company *Echo Bay Mines.*

In 1995, 26-year-old employee Nick Leeson single-handedly brought down *Barings*, Britain's oldest bank. His secret unauthorized trading deals caused losses of £827 million ($1.6 billion) – twice the bank's available trading capital.

In 1996, McDonald's opened the first 'ski-thru' restaurant in Sälen, Sweden.

In 1996, Bangkok police had a tip-off about a bomb in the toilets of Thailand's Parliament. A search revealed a box containing not a bomb but a huge monitor lizard!

In the 1990s, Zagreb airport in Croatia began using birds of prey to clear the airport of small birds that might collide with planes, causing accidents.

The first ever space funeral took place on 9 February 1997. The ashes of several famous Americans – including *Star Trek* creator Gene Roddenberry and writer and psychologist Timothy Leary – were placed aboard a *Pegasus* rocket and fired into space.

It cost $200 million (about £101 million) to make the movie *Titanic* in 1997, but it would cost only $123 million (about £61 million) to build the ship today.

The first-ever space vote was cast in November 1997. Astronaut David Wolf emailed his vote for the mayor of Houston while aboard the Russian space station *Mir*. Texas is the only state in the USA that permits residents to vote from space.

The longest-living person in history was Jeanne Calment, a woman from Arles, France, who lived 122 years from 1875 to 1997.

The internet search engine, *Google,* was founded in 1998 in California, USA. The name is a misspelling of the word *googol* (the number '1' followed by 100 zeros), reflecting the company's mission to organize the immense amount of information available online.

On 9 May 1999, some 2.2 million litres (600,000 gallons) of whiskey poured into the Kentucky River during a fire at the Wild Turkey Distillery in Lawrenceburg, Kentucky. The fish must have felt a bit funny!

Many different groups predicted that the world would end once the year 2000 (the new millennium) began... well, we're still here so they were all wrong!

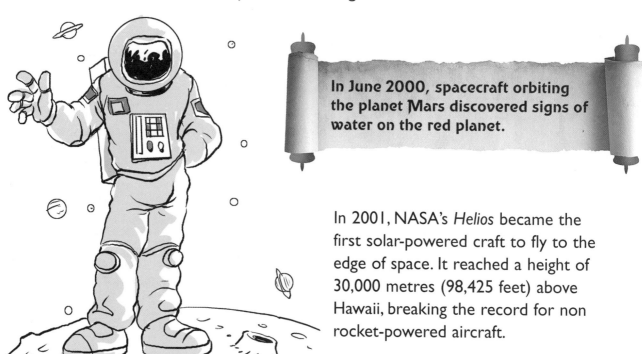

In June 2000, spacecraft orbiting the planet Mars discovered signs of water on the red planet.

In 2001, NASA's *Helios* became the first solar-powered craft to fly to the edge of space. It reached a height of 30,000 metres (98,425 feet) above Hawaii, breaking the record for non rocket-powered aircraft.

The first 'zombie walk' took place in 2001 in a shopping centre in Sacramento, California. In a zombie walk, people dress as the walking dead and invade a shopping centre as a protest against consumerism.

In 2003, the Human Genome Project was completed. It revealed that the human blueprint contains between 30,000 and 40,000 genes, but there were some very strange discoveries... It found that we have only twice as many genes as a *fruitfly*, and share many genes with plants and animals. One scientist said, 'It comes as a shock to discover that you are 60 per cent banana!'

In 2003, a burglar in Oslo, Norway, broke into a flat. Unknown to him, the flat was being used to film the Norwegian version of the reality television show *Big Brother*. Seventeen video cameras recorded his every move and the whole crime was shown in real time over the internet.

In 2005, a Japanese inventor devised solar-powered clothes, which can top up the battery on an iPod or mobile phone.

In the USA, more toy *Monopoly* money is printed every day than real currency.